Bless You Richly!

[illegible]

5/99

#1

RELUCTANT RAINBOWS

A Personal Journey
from
Failure to Freedom

By
Dale Crawshaw

Published by
WisdomPress
- a ministry of WisdomSeekers, International -
Atlanta, Georgia

Bible References
The New International Version
Zondervan Publishing
Grand Rapids, Michigan
Used by Permission

Dedication

This book is lovingly dedicated
to my remarkable mom, "Miss Lou",
who was known and loved by everyone she met.

Her funeral service
was a standing room only celebration.
She lived out before me
the "how to" of never giving up -
no matter how difficult the adversity,
or how destructive the storm.
She laughed at the days to come
and handled every chapter of her life
with an optimistic spirit.
She is on every page of "Reluctant Rainbows".

Many thanks to my publishing team,
Gordon Lawrence
Dick Sauer
Beth Wilson,
who have truly made this book
their own labor of love.

Foreword

The rainbow is a curious scientific phenomenon. It first occurred during the time of Noah, immediately after the waters of The Great Flood had engulfed the earth. The human population had perished, except for Noah and his family, and God used a rainbow as the symbol of His faithfulness to mankind.

Genesis 9:13-17

I have set my rainbow in the clouds,
and it will be the sign of the covenant
between me and the earth.
Whenever I bring clouds over the earth
and the rainbow appears in the clouds,
I will remember my covenant between me and you
and all living creatures of every kind.
Never again will the waters
become a flood to destroy all life.
Whenever the rainbow appears in the clouds,
I will see it and remember the everlasting covenant
between God and all living creatures
of every kind on the earth.

Not only was the rainbow important in the early days of man's existence, but Bible prophecy tells us that the rainbow will actually supersede human history to be a part of God's eternal kingdom.

Revelation 4:3

And the one who sat there
had the appearance of jasper and carnelian.
A rainbow, resembling an emerald, encircled the throne.

In this book, Dale Crawshaw chronicles his personal story of tragedies and triumphs, of successes and failures.

Ultimately, Dale concludes that God could only use his personal failures in life to bring him to a point of fulfillment. Dale Crawshaw has truly become a model of triumph for me. If the apostle Paul were to search the earth today for another Barnabas, a "Son of Encouragement", I think he would find that person in Dale. The world is crying out for real life models of virtue, humility, transparency and vulnerability. I believe Dale is a worthy candidate for our attention as he vividly tracks the agony and ecstasy of the human dilemma.

Reluctant Rainbows is a creative way of describing the process God uses to reveal His brilliant display of majesty in our lives, often at the point of struggling first through the dark clouds and storms of desperation.

There is a wealth of scripture to be found in this book. Dale's attention to Biblical principles and his breadth of referencing Biblical characters will make this a book that you will reference a second and third time after you've read it once.

As of this writing, Dale continues to hope and pray for a kidney transplant to add years to his life. With great courage and silent suffering, this former all star athlete now quietly endures his own personal battle while simultaneously lifting up and encouraging those around him who need to hear a voice of calm assurance.

Dale paints a real life portrait
of the illusion of success
and the fulfillment resulting in failure.
After all, failure is just another way
of pointing us to dependence on God,
which ultimately brings us back to
the reality of success.

- Gordon Lawrence -

Blessed
is any weight,
however overwhelming,
which God
has been so good
as to fasten
with His own hand
upon our shoulders.

F.W. Faber

Contents

"WHOA-AA, THIS ISN'T EXACTLY WHAT I HAD IN MIND WHEN I JUMPED OUT OF THE BOAT!"

Introduction

It was a warm beautiful day in the Florida Keys where I was raised. Alone with fellow high school juniors Lee and Jay, I had just donned scuba diving gear and would momentarily be spearfishing above a breathtaking coral reef. I had an uneasy feeling in my stomach about the dive. My friend Scottie and his dad had recently been attacked and killed by a shark after their boat capsized on the reef just three miles to the north.

The water was chilly, but tolerable, and we were soon absorbed in pursuing one of the biggest grouper I had ever seen. The big fellow finally disappeared into an underwater cave. We found ourselves on the far edge of the reef with the oxygen in our scuba tanks depleted. As we surfaced we noticed that the wind had intensified and the waves were much larger than when we entered the water. All of this made the one-half mile surface swim back to the boat difficult and tiring.

But something much more terrifying than white-capped waves was to touch our lives that day. It was nothing unusual to see a shark in the reef area or even to be underwater with one. They generally minded their business and you warily minded yours. This one, though, was different. For one thing, it was big. It looked, in fact, more like a small submarine! And to our terror, this shark began swimming in a pattern we called "the kill circle," typical of a hungry shark stalking its prey.

The distance to the boat looked like a thousand miles. The three of us wrapped our arms around each other as we swam, hoping we would appear too large a prey for the shark to attack. You can imagine the thoughts that ran through my mind as we swam numbly toward our boat. The shark kept circling, ever so slowly tightening its circle.

After what seemed like an eternity of swimming we reached the boat only to encounter another problem. The boat was bouncing so forcefully in the heavy seas that we had to dump our heavy diving gear into the sea - gone forever - to give us the mobility to climb aboard. This we did as the shark now circled both us and the boat! With trembling hands Jay hurriedly cut the anchor rope and we bolted toward dry land.

As the boat skimmed across the waves toward the shoreline my mind was wired with thoughts - many having to do with death and eternity. In that crucial encounter, I told God that I would like to know Him better and do something with my life for Him.

God must delight in responding to those kinds of requests. For in but a few short weeks I was to become part of a whole new world. It all started with an encounter with Lee's step-brother, Roy. Roy was what some people would call a religious fanatic, always carrying his Bible and talking about the Lord. After our day of terror Roy found us in quite a listening mood.

How well I remember the night that he showed me from the Bible a wonderful thing Christ had done for me; how Jesus had made a payment in full for my sins by His death on Calvary's cross. Surely it couldn't be so simple! Through the entire night I asked questions and Roy showed me answers out of the Bible. Finally, I ran out of questions. Needless to say, the Bible had not run out of answers. As the sun was rising above the peaceful Florida Bay I acknowledged to Him my sinful condition and asked the Lord Jesus Christ to forgive me of my sins. What an exciting, thoroughly cleansing and indescribable experience that was! A few weeks later I asked my heavenly Father to use my life in a special way for His glory. How little did I know what was in store for me!

Loneliness.
Despondency.
Desperation.

These feelings engulf the one who has hit "rock bottom."

Failing, and especially failing often, or at something vitally important, is ironically somewhat like being caught underwater with a hungry shark. For along with being overwhelmed with fright, one cannot help but experience many other poignant emotions. There is that almost-impossible-to-describe loneliness . . . that gripping despondency . . . that paralyzing desperation. These and many other feelings engulf the life of anyone who is seeing the world from a “rock bottom” viewpoint. These are the type of events we feel uncomfortable talking about. These are experiences we would like to block from memory. These are troubles we feel hesitant unburdening even to a committed Christian friend.

First of all, let's stop avoiding the issue. One guy told me this: "I know I need to read your book but I'm just too proud to pick up a book that has the word failure on the front cover." C'mon, fella! Get real. We've all messed up, and most of us have messed up big time! We're talking about moving from failure to freedom. But, hey, we don't have to wallow in it. We're talking about experiencing a level of spiritual dynamics in life we might not have ever tasted if it weren't for our failures!

And guess what else? God has some absolutely astounding and life changing principles waiting for us to experience through what can be one of life's greatest "blessings in disguise" - failure! So come with me and experience a part of my life's journey. After thirty plus years of being in His Kingdom I wish I could tell you that I've officially retired from failing. I wish I could tell you I've learned all the lessons there are to learn from it. Not so. I'm still learning about the spiritual dynamics of those times in my life that I really messed up. I can't wait to tell you just how wonderful those rainbows are after the storm.

"THE JAILHOUSE OF DEFEAT"
"DISCOURAGED FAILURES ALWAYS WELCOME!"
MAKE IT RIGHT TOMORROW
PAST FAILURES ALWAYS VISIT AGAIN!!
WE'VE SERVED OUR TIME HON, LET'S START LIVING BY FAITH... NO SENSE IN BEING IMPRISONED TO DEFEAT WITH A GOD AS BIG AS OURS!!!

Chapter One

Discovering the Success in Failure

Seven years had passed since that dramatic, life-changing "Christmas shark encounter." Absorbing, event-filled years. Years when God's clear direction led me to, and through, rewarding college and seminary experiences as I moved toward a Christian ministry career.

Marriage to Rachel also enriched those years. She was a wonderful midwestern girl with a burning desire to be totally given to, and used of God.

What more could one ask? Seven years filled with what most people would have termed "plenty of success"! Atlanta, a city I still love, had become my home - my launching pad for ministry career dreams. Dreams which rode high on the momentum of past experiences till I thought the world surely was waiting for me with open arms. Not so! In fact, I was soon thrust into the painful realization that the world was quite oblivious to all of that youthful optimism. And reality certainly wasted no time in engulfing me in its ruthless claws!

CRISIS IN THE MATERNITY WARD

Stabbed awake by the telephone's piercing ring, I squinted at the clock. Five a.m.! Retracing the evening before, my sleepy mind recalled the doctor's statement that the chances of Rachel's giving birth to a very premature child were quite slim. So strong was his assurance that I had felt free to leave my wife at the hospital and return home for some much needed rest.

By now, the phone was in its sixth ring. Stumbling out of bed, I stepped on, of all things, a most irate little scorpion. The surprise was worse than the sting! And instead of a sleepy "hello," the startled nurse on the other end recoiled from a howling "ouch!" She must have wondered why I too was not hospitalized! But her emergency trained voice spoke calmly and gave me an update on the situation.

Yes, our own first child had been born! Rejoicing was short-lived, however, because little Julia's arrival into the world was far from picture perfect. Almost three months premature, she weighed barely three pounds and was destined to experience some serious problems.

Several times during her first few days Julia stopped breathing and had to be revived by "divinely" alerted nurses. And the doctor gravely informed us that if our daughter did live there would be a chance of brain damage.

For weeks tiny Julia lay in an isolette, tubes gently attached to her delicate veins. Her tiny body was engulfed by my hand as I stroked her little back to assure her of our love. Weeks of uncertainty and conflicting medical reports were to pass before she could be brought home.

Yet that traumatic birth was just the leading edge of the avalanche of events God had prepared for me. Sorrow was to strike some weeks later, when my mother's sudden death overwhelmed me with a painful, gnawing emptiness.

Enough, you say? Not yet. Shortly after my mother's death, my treasured, fulfilling youth ministry position was abruptly terminated. No ministry. No money. No friends. A precarious little baby. Lingering grief from the loss of a precious loved one. They all moved with us - into a tiny, hot apartment! Talk about a rude awakening!

> *"My thoughts are not your thoughts,*
> *neither are your ways my ways, saith the LORD."*
>
> **Isaiah 55:8**

TAILOR MADE FOR SUCCESS

Tailor-made for success . . . that's what I had been called. My college president often teased me that I could succeed at anything that could be organized or promoted. Organize? Promote? Yes, but what if suddenly there's nothing even to consider organizing? Past successes were meaningless - whisked into life's fleeting memories. For the first time in my life there was literally nothing - nothing of that elusive thing called success. And what an unwelcome shock that was!

Success. Just what is it? Webster's defines it as *". . . obtaining what one desires or intends; especially having reached a high degree of worldly prosperity".* Right on - from the world's viewpoint! Get what you intend to get from life! That's success, right?

On the other hand, what about failure? Again from Webster's *". . . to be lacking or deficient, as in ability, energy, loyalty, etc. - to leave undone or unfulfilled."* Man's definition of failure, then, is a person's inability to achieve his desired goals.

These are good definitions . . . by the world's standards! The system of human logic in which most people operate says that success is accomplishing that which you set out to do. And failure is to leave undone or to fail while attempting that which you felt you ought to have achieved.

Yes, man judges success on outward appearances. A good job, an attractive family, a nice home, an outgoing personality - convincing even to most Christians. Yet we read that God is looking at matters quite differently. He searches the heart, the motives, the inward character. 1 Samuel 16:7 says, "Man looks on the outward appearances, but God looks at the heart."

Wait a minute! Is it unspiritual to be successful? Is someone a failure just because he is not measuring up to the world's standards? Can I not learn my lessons and continue to grow spiritually without becoming a miserable earthly loser?

Men want only the strong,
the successful,
the victorious,
the unbroken,
in building their kingdoms;

But God is the God
of the unsuccessful,
of those who have failed.
Heaven is being filled
with earth's broken lives,
and there is no bruised reed
that Christ cannot take
and restore
to glorious blessedness
and beauty.

J.R. Miller

Right! Worldly success is neither unspiritual nor necessarily unhealthy. And yes, one can grow spiritually through response to God's goodness and continued obedience to His Word. So very often, however, God must allow us to fail - and sometimes miserably so - in order to, as a starter, get our undivided attention. Which is exactly why we cannot judge anyone's spiritual progress (including our own) by the world's standards!

VIEWED BY THE WORLD AS FAILURES

Remember the king who seemed to really have "his act together"? Physically this man stood head and shoulders above the rest of the people. The cream of the crop, the top of the line. Yes, he was the man for the people. He was the king! And, **King Saul** may have passed his earthly evaluations with flying colors. But not so with God; for God was gravely disappointed with the "real Saul."

Or how about the opposite end of the spectrum? Like **Job**, whose friends and relatives wrote him off as a misguided evil-doer - failure if there ever was one. Yet God commended him!

Solomon. Ah! Here we have it! King Solomon - wisdom, prestige, possessions, pleasure - as much as any human being could experience. A unanimous candidate for success by this world's standards! But as life whisked by and Solomon looked back upon his innumerable successes, he despondently described it all in one simple phrase: "Meaningless! Meaningless . . . Everything is meaningless!" (Ecclesiastes 12:8)

Rahab's past life was one of harlotry - the lowest occupations in every society. Automatic and final condemnation should be her lot - right? "Wrong!" says God who saw fit, from His Divine perspective, to include her name in Hebrews 11 right along with many of the other great men and women of dynamic faith.

Ridiculed, doubted, disobeyed, disowned by the majority of thousands - the very thousands he was commissioned to lead. That was **Moses** - the same man whose close relationship with

God has never been equaled. But let's move on - closer to home. Like the past century . . .

Adoniram Judson was a pioneer missionary to Burma. Did you know that he was disowned and discredited by his supporters because his first seven years of ministry in the "heathen" country produced only one convert? Yet today his Burmese translation of the Bible is a welcome tool for hundreds of missionaries!

Now here's an interesting group of people. I wonder what man's description of them would be...

Hudson Taylor
scoffed at by fellow workers and clergy,

George Mueller
often considered insane.

Dwight L. Moody
branded a heretic.

David Livingston
given up as a feeble, helpless old man.

Mary Slessor
written off as "out of the will of God."

Amy Carmichael
turned upon by fellow workers.

Failures! All failures! Really? Is that what God says? Does

He have a "rest of the story" for these and countless other wasted lives? Yes! He does! A story being told today by the living descendants of the multitude of lives these failures influenced for the cause of Christ.

Surely the "great cloud of witnesses" (Hebrews 12:1,2) of God's children down through the ages who have perhaps failed in man's eyes while succeeding in the sight of God ought to be a special encouragement to us. An absolute assurance that the only score card that really matters is the record of those things that count eternally. "For we must all appear before the judgment seat of Christ, that each one may receive what is due him for the things done while in the body, whether good or bad." (2 Corinthians 5:10)

"the only scorecard that really matters is the record of those things that count eternally."

Glorifying God in every circumstance or event that life brings our way - is that not true success? And shouldn't our time, our talents, our energy, our resources and our very being be consumed with doing just that? Giving God opportunity to show His goodness and His greatness on our behalf - what a blessed lifestyle! "Call unto Me and I will answer you and show you great and unsearchable things you do not know." (Jeremiah 33:3) And you know what? God's children are uniquely eligible for just that kind of victorious life! God gives us warning and blessing in Psalm, chapter one . . .

"Blessed is the man who does not walk in the counsel of the wicked or stand in the way of sinners or sit in the seat of mockers. But his delight is in the law of the Lord, and on his law he meditates day and night. He is like a tree planted by streams of water, which yields its fruit in season and whose leaf does not wither. Whatever he does prospers." (Psalm 1:1-3)

Another verse which defines God's perspective on success is found in the instruction to Joshua. "Do not let this Book of the law depart from your mouth; meditate on it day and night, so that you may be careful to do everything written in it. Then you will be prosperous and successful." (Joshua 1:8)

VIEWED BY GOD AS SUCCESS

If it is so good and right and blessed to prosper, why do we see so many apparent experiences of failure in the lives of great saints? Remember **Joseph,** spiritually dynamic even as a youth, who was sold into slavery, thrown into prison and totally forgotten for years? None was ever more humble before the Lord than **Moses** - the same Moses who spent one-third of his life as a lowly herdsman!

Abraham was called the very friend of God - yet was he not the man who earlier told grave lies which indicated doubt of God's watchcare? Had he not delayed in obeying God's leading? Had he not tried but miserably failed in his own ingenuity to fulfill God's promise of a son?

Or how about **Ezra**, who spent most of his life in prison? Or **Nehemiah**, a mere slave to a king? Or **Ruth**, who lost her people, husband, father-in-law, material possessions? Or **David**, who committed adultery, ordered a murder, suffered betrayal by his own son, acted insane through fear for his life, saw many of his sons and daughters turn from the Lord? Or **Jeremiah**, who spent a lifetime trying to share God's truths with a people who refused to "hear and heed" even a word of it!

Remember **Mary Magdalene**? She was labeled a demon possessed harlot, despised by the "righteous" of her day. Yet that same Mary demonstrated unwavering commitment to her Savior. **Matthew** was greedy and despised, as were all the tax collectors of his day. But our Lord chose him as one of the twelve who would be the foundation of the spreading of His cause. Brash **Peter** dared to rebuke, challenge and deny Christ, only to be used by that same Jesus as a key figure in turning the world upside down for Christianity.

Paul. Yes, Paul - stoned, shipwrecked, imprisoned, deserted often by fellow believers, hunted as a wild beast, after receiving no material support for his dedicated service. Dare we doubt that he was a spiritual success?

We've just touched the surface on the tremendously reassuring evidence God has left us in His Word. Assurance that our failures today, yesterday - or even a lifetime of them - cannot be interpreted as proof of failure tomorrow. What is the key - there must be one - that separates those who continue to live in a general state of spiritual failure from those who fail, yet ultimately become spiritually prosperous?

Response. That's the key. One simple word. But it makes all the difference between a lifetime of failure and ever increasing spiritual maturity. How one responds to life's onslaughts of defeat and failure has everything to do with whether that life becomes a miracle of God's inexhaustible grace . . . or a needless waste of bitterness and despair.

My experiences in failure - and you will soon see that this author has had several good doses of it - have taught me some remarkable things. As I travel and share with friends around the nation I constantly find that failure is found everywhere. In fact, an astounding number of Christians would label themselves lifelong failures. And that is alarming. Alarming, not because so many have failed at so much but because so many have failed to profit from their failures. In order to learn to profit from failure, we must first understand it. We must understand God's principles of handling failure. We must believe that there truly is a spiritual dynamics in failure! In this study we will take a careful look at three vital areas of our Christian growth as they relate to failure.

However, we need to answer three questions:

First, what are the common areas of failure and failure related dilemmas the Christian will likely experience during his lifetime?

Second, what is God desiring to teach His child in each of life's "difficult places"?

Third, how would God have us respond to the various trials, testings and failures we will inevitably experience in this life?

In other words: What in the world is happening to me? Why in the world is it happening to me? And, how in the world am I to respond to, and change, because of these happenings? It seems that God is always our last resort.

In a nutshell, what God wants us to learn from the His Word and from our personal experience, is that God's marvelous grace is sufficient to bring about great victories through devastating defeats.

For what God wants to make out of His children through failure is exciting! It's fantastic! It's beyond our earthly comprehension. That's why it is indeed vital that we try to learn and understand and apply what He is doing through life's hard spots. Remembering that His work in our lives is prompted by an unfathomable love for us - and carried out in the multitude of His tender mercies. "Answer me, 0 Lord, out of the goodness of your love; in your great mercy turn to me." (Psalm 69:16)

When our Lord shared with us His supernatural ability to give not only life, but to give it "more abundantly," (Ephesians 3:20) was He talking about the run-of-the-mill, "just slide through another year of existence"? The kind most people are experiencing? Not at all. He had in mind a life "in this world" yet "not of this world." A life that would not be plummeted into defeat and despair by the circumstances all of us must invariably experience.

Still it seems that the harder we strive to experience that kind of miraculous, victory filled, way of life . . . the harder life seems to get.

Those rainbows do come reluctantly, don't they?

CHAPTER ONE
Scriptural Insights

1. I Samuel 16:7b

   Man judges on outward appearance, but God looks at inner motives.

2. Ecclesiastes 1: 17, 18

   The frustrations of the wisdom of this world.

3. Isaiah 55:8, 9

   God's thoughts and ways are beyond our deepest comprehension.

4. I Corinthians 1:25-31

   God often uses losers in this world as instruments of His cause.

5. Colossians 3:23

   We are instructed to live the Christian life to its fullest potential.

6. Matthew 23:25-27

   Outward righteousness is no sure indicator of inward spirituality.

7. Psalm 119:161-168

   God's Word has the answer for every problem or distress.

8. I Corinthians 2:1-16

   The indwelling Spirit of God supplies us with supernatural abilities.

9. Psalm 119:9-16
   Knowing and applying God's Word discourages sin and brings joy.

10. I Kings 1-10
    Solomon, desiring God's wisdom above all else, is greatly blessed.

11. I Samuel 13:13-14
    Saul's kingdom to be removed because of faithless attitudes.

12. Job 42:7
    God rebukes Job's friends for wrongly judging Job.

13. Ecclesiastes 12:8
    Solomon's bleak summary of a life not lived for God.

14. Hebrews 11:31
    Rahab's faith allowed God to work supernaturally in her life.

15. Numbers 12:3
    God records for us His opinion of Moses' humility.

16. Hebrews 12:1, 2
    We are to patiently endure life's tribulations because of the heavenly hope that lies ahead.

17. II Corinthians 5:10
    All believers must someday appear before the Lord for judgment of earthly actions.

18. Ephesians 2:7
God's majestic design is that we begin to comprehend His goodness to us.

19. Ephesians 3:20
God is able to do in our lives more than we could possibly imagine.

20. Psalm 1:1-3
Loving and meditating on God's Word means strength and true success.

21. Jeremiah 33:3
God's ability to work miraculously in our lives is clearly stated.

22. Joshua 1:8
Obedience to God's Word brings prosperity and success.

23. III John 2
Health and prosperity can be related to our spiritual health.

24. Psalm 69:16
God's promised response to our plea for His supernatural ministry in our lives is given.

25. John 10:10
Christ's promise to us for a miraculously abundant life

Let's Get Personal !

1. In your own words,
define success from a human perspective.

2. Reference one verse of scripture
which indicates that God's idea of success
is different from man's.

3. Now reference one verse of scripture
that defines God's view of "real" success.

"I DON'T KNOW WHY IT'S SO HARD TO MAKE IT TO THE TOP IN LIFE... BUT I'M GONNA GET THERE IF IT KILLS ME!"
HIS WAY BLVD.
MY WAY AVE.
ROAD CLOSED

Chapter Two

The Harder I Try The Behinder I Get

Starting a college is a mammoth undertaking. At age twenty two, most of my contemporaries were just graduating from college, but here I was trying to establish a new educational institution. In spite of all the disheartening experiences of family problems (my mother's death and daughter's birth), I was still filled with unbounded youthful optimism. Once again I was ready to tackle the impossible.

During my two years of youth ministry it had become evident to several key Christian leaders that the need for a quality Christian college in the Atlanta area could be no longer denied. The problem was that no one had taken the "bull by the horns" to get the project initiated. I just knew that I was to be God's instrument to spearhead that project.

Day and night the seemingly endless details were tediously researched. The entire catalog was written, including course descriptions, majors, electives and general policies. Several outstanding educators from across the country had already been interviewed for the positions of president and dean. Preliminary funding had been secured. In spite of the resistance of ministers to something new - an impressive group of pastors had expressed enough interest in the college to attend several lengthy planning meetings.

One well-known pastor had expressed a keen interest in the project. I began to spend hours with him outlining ideas, looking at prospective facilities, discussing potential professors and charting enrollment projections. Amidst all of this planning I was also earning my masters degree and teaching in a Christian school. It looked as though I was back in the groove of "obtaining what one desires or intends" that I had previously enjoyed. And, for eighteen months, the project clearly seemed to be gaining momentum.

But one early morning breakfast engagement was sadly to be the first stage of reversing that momentum. The pastor I had been depending upon so heavily regretfully informed me that he had been offered, and was accepting the position of president of an out of town Christian university. He would publicly withdraw his support from the project. What a devastating blow that turned out to be!

With the pastor's interest abruptly removed, community interest in the project steadily declined.

He gives more grace
when the burdens grow greater,
He sends more strength
when the labors increase;
To added affliction
He addeth His mercies,
To multiplied trials
His multiplied peace.

When we have exhausted
our store of endurance,
When our strength has failed
ere the day is half done,
When we reach the end
of our hoarded resources
Our Father's full giving
is only begun.

Annie Johnson Flint

It was like I was swimming upstream with the current moving more and more rapidly against me! It finally became quite evident that momentum had settled at ground zero. Two years of hard work left me with twenty-five photocopies of a catalog, a file full of ideas and one very crushed dream.

FRUSTRATION UNLIMITED

Indeed, it did seem that the harder I tried the faster things were moving . . . in reverse! And, not just with the college but with everything.

Little Julia may have been small of stature but she was mighty of willpower. It seemed apparent that having to fight to survive as an infant had given her a feisty, stubborn stamina. She fought gum and nail, then, tooth and nail and, finally, teeth and nail to get her way in every imaginable circumstance!

You couldn't have convinced me that tender love and tough discipline were phasing her in the least. And with a second child on the way, I was beginning to ask myself, "Is this what I went to four years of college for? Is this what I call a purpose in life? Does this have anything at all to do with turning the world upside down for Jesus Christ?"

To make matters more bewildering, Rachel's new record album (my wife has recorded several albums) had gotten mis-blended in the final "mix" at the recording studio. The albums were pressed and shipped to us before this was discovered. And would you believe it, the recording studio had erased the master tape with all the original recordings! We spent many a late evening imaginatively thinking of all the things we could make "the harder I tried, the faster things moved . . . in reverse!"

out of melted and remolded record albums. Perhaps we would start a frisbee distribution company! Or maybe they could even be melted and molded into toy blocks for kids!

"Why, Lord? We just want to serve you. We just want to do a special work for you; to be used as your instruments as you see fit. Why these seemingly endless dead-end streets?"

Why are we so often greeted by dead-end streets in our efforts to do His will? Is He up there simply thinking of ways to make life frustrating for His own children? Is this whole thing we call living some kind of joke on mankind?

Or, could it be that God is trying to tell us something? Could it be that without those rock-bottom failures our lives would be robbed of a wonderfully vital ingredient?

ELIJAH AND THE PROPHETS OF BAAL

Remember Elijah's remarkable experience as the key human instrument in the Lord's overwhelming victory over the prophets of Baal and Ashtaroth? Eight hundred fifty of those false prophets had howled and screamed, and slashed themselves with stones trying to persuade their gods to make themselves known to thousands of onlookers - all to not even a whisper of a response. Elijah's bold request: " 'Answer me, 0 Lord; answer me, so these people will know that you, 0 Lord, are God, and that you are turning their hearts back again.' Then the fire of the Lord fell, and burned up the sacrifice, the wood, the stones and the soil, and also licked up the water in the trench." (1 Kings 18:37-38)

What a fantastic victory - only to be followed the very next day by an equally astounding defeat. A most infuriated Queen Jezebel informed Elijah that not only did she ill-appreciate his exterminating all of her precious prophets - but that she fully intended to exterminate him!

What do you think Elijah did? Why, he was terrified of that insanely irate woman and fled for his life! After several weeks of seclusion in the wilderness, Elijah, full of self-pity, was asked by God why he was hiding. Elijah was convinced that other than himself there was no one else left in Israel who would take a stand for the Lord. " I am the only one left, and now they are trying to kill me too." (1 Kings 19:10c)

Now that statement caused quite a reaction from the Lord. God immediately responded to Elijah's "human reasoning" with a tumultuous wind, a mighty earthquake and a blazing fire. Unquestionably the Lord now had Elijah's undivided attention! And scripture goes on to say that in a "gentle whisper" God began to give the despondent prophet new direction. What looked like the end of the line was transformed into an opportunity for God to work wonderfully in Elijah's life - To minister to his weakened faith. To encourage him to forget that which was behind. To reach for that which was yet to be done.

Have you ever come face to face with no small number of life's roadblocks? Have you been trapped in what seems like an ocean of hopeless failure and defeat?

SITE OF ELIJAH'S GOD-
WROUGHT VICTORY OVER
THE FALSE PROPHETS OF
BAAL & ASHEROTAL
I'VE GOT TO GET OUT OF HERE PRONTO BEFORE THAT CRAZY LADY EXTERMINATES ME!

Like Elijah, have you found yourself retreating from reality, sure that no one really understands the pressures that are overwhelming your inner being? As God tenderly ministered to Elijah, He desires to touch your life today. For when you exhaust your resources, realizing that your human stamina is inadequate for combat in life's intense spiritual warfare, remember to listen for that still small voice.

RUTH

Ruth's life, too, appeared to be run over by insurmountable odds. Her husband and father-in-law had just died. The country in which she lived was plagued by a terrible famine. Her mother-in-law, Naomi, pleaded with her to return to her own kinsfolk to salvage some kind of reasonable life for herself.

And, seemingly, Ruth had a right to look out for her own well-being and future. Had she not experienced enough meaningless heartache already? Was she not at "the end of herself"? Surely, any practical solution to her desperate predicament would be the right thing to do! The logical way out was not God's design for Ruth's life, though!

Scripture records this amazing sequence of events, "Then Orpah (Ruth's sister-in-law) kissed her mother-in-law goodbye, but Ruth clung to her. 'Look,' said Naomi (her mother-in-law), 'your sister-in-law is going back to her people and her gods. Go back with her.' But Ruth replied, 'Don't urge me to leave you or to turn back from you. Where you go I will go, and where you stay I will stay. Your people will be my people and your God my God. Where you die I will die, and there I will be buried. May the Lord deal with me, be it ever so severely, if anything but death separates you and me." (Ruth 1:14-17)

A dead-end street? A life of despair and good reason for lifelong bitterness? No hope for a brighter tomorrow? Not so with Ruth! Neither did the character that was being instilled in her life go unnoticed. For, through a miraculous series of events she was not only to become the wife of a wonderful, God-fearing man but to be the great grandmother of King David as well!

What was so special about Ruth? Godward response! Rather than wilt under the pressures of life and take the human way out, she sought the wisdom, and strength of an infinitely resourceful Lord. Yes, life had undeniably caved in around her. Any on-looker would have viewed her life as one of failure or, at best, grave misfortune. Ruth could easily have reasoned, "God surely hasn't given me anything to live for. I suppose I should go back to my people. That will surely be better than what I've already been through!"

She refused to slip into grasping at that first "ray of human hope". She would not allow her inward emotional feelings - though they must surely have been pulsating - to dictate her decision making. It was that inner discipline which allowed life's hurts, losses and disappointments to build within her that special kind of character which we call today Christlikeness. That quality which allows God the opportunity to work in our behalf, to bless us. "Call to Me and I will answer you and tell you great and unsearchable things you do not know." (Jeremiah 33:3)

It was an often "backed into the corner" David who was moved of God to pen these inspired words, "In my anguish I cried to the Lord, and he answered by setting me free. The Lord is with me; I will not be afraid. What can man do to me? The Lord is with me; he is my helper. I will look in triumph on my enemies. It is better to take refuge in the Lord than to trust in princes." (Psalm 118:5-9)

Could it be that "the harder we seem to work at something the behinder we get" experiences of life are God's way of revealing something vital to us? Is He not graciously telling us that He is interested in showing Himself strong in our helplessness? Doesn't He desire to take a defeated, exhausted child of His and make something miraculous out of that life? Is it possible we would never come to a place of day-by-day dependence upon Him if the security blankets of life had not been tugged from our ever-clutching grasp? "Before I was afflicted I went astray, but now I obey your word. It was good for me to be afflicted, so that I might learn your decrees." (Psalm 119)

Years after the episode of failing to start a new college I was blessed with a remarkable insight from a wise old saint. In describing successful Christian living he simply, but profoundly, stated, **"I can't do it. He can. And He will - if I'll let Him!"**

As long as I am in the way, trying by my own strength and self will to make by life what I think it ought to be, I am actually hindering God's "freedom" to work through me.

What is so devastating in the life of a Christian who is pulling, tugging, straining, and conniving to be in the driver's seat of his life? It's pride! That's the problem. It's pride which subtly convinces us that we indeed can successfully run our own lives. Of course, God is not left out of the picture - for we reason that we can always call on Him when we really need Him!

We see that by His own decree God must oppose - must come against vehemently - any child of His in the areas of his life where self-will, conceit and self-determination are more dominant than the leadership of His Spirit. Pride has aptly been called "the number one roadblock to true spiritual success." "Young men, in the same way be submissive to those who are older. All of you, clothe yourselves with humility toward one another, because, 'God opposes the proud but gives grace to the humble.' Humble yourselves, therefore, under God's mighty hand, that he may lift you up in due time." (1 Peter 5:5)

In a very real sense you must first become poor in spirit - even to the point of utter despair - before you are ready to receive and enjoy the spiritual riches that only Christ can give.

Pride is exactly why so often God must allow us, through a seemingly endless variety of trials, tribulations, heartaches and failures, to reach the end of our own resources. To bring us to the point of having exhausted our tenacious ambitions that we might forever realize the futility of doing it our way. And some of us have quite a storehouse of that self-will that needs to be weeded out!

I am convinced that when we get to heaven - if we are permitted to look back at our earthly lives - one of the areas which we will thank our Lord most will be His unwavering resistance to our self-willed plans and efforts to run our lives.

Imagine the futuristic cinema in which we witness what a horrifying disaster our lives would become had not God created many roadblocks and hard spots! Failures we experienced brought us to a greater dependence upon Him. Ultimately the failures brought us success by His standards.

So we are faced with a vital choice. Will we spend a lifetime working in cooperation with God's Spirit as He creatively chooses? Or, will we cling to the “right" to pursue success our way - stubbornly ignoring God's efforts to make our human vessel wholly usable for His Spirit's leadership?

As He remolded “sure" defeat into glorious victory in the lives of Ruth and the thousands of similar people, He can do it for you! You can’t do it. I can't do it. He can! And, yes, He will if we allow Him the opportunity simply to live His life through us!

"I have been crucified with Christ and I no longer live, but Christ lives in me. The life I live in the body, I live by faith in the Son of God, who loved me and gave himself for me.” (Galatians 2:20)

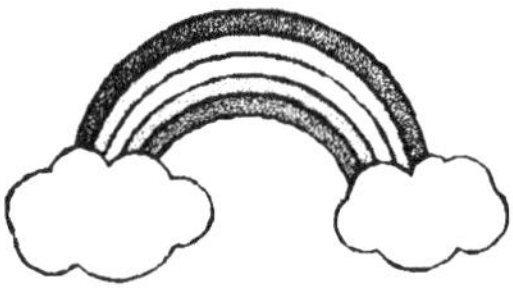

I can still believe
that a day comes for all of us,
however far off it may be,
when we shall understand;
when these tragedies
that now blacken and darken
the very air of heaven for us
will sink into their places
in a scheme so august,
so magnificent,
so joyful, that we shall laugh
for wonder and delight.

Arthur Christopher Benson

CHAPTER TWO
Scriptural Insights

1. I Kings 18:37-38
   God proves Himself as the Almighty One.

2. I Kings 19:10c
   Elijah lapses into self-pity and doubt.

3. I Kings 19:12
   God gently ministers to Elijah's broken spirit

4. Ruth 1:14-17
   Ruth makes a no-turning-back commitment to do what she believed God would have her do.

5. I Kings 19:10c
   Elijah lapses into self-pity and doubt.

6. Psalm 118:5-9
   No human source can meet our needs as can the Lord.

7. Psalm 119:67, 71
   The pressures of life caused the psalmist to adhere to Him.

8. Philippians 3:7-14
   Those things which benefit me humanly, invariably add up to spiritual loss.

9. Hebrews 4:9-10

The believer has the unique opportunity to experience an incomprehensible peace because of God's power at work in his behalf.

10. Hebrews 11:33-40

Christian history proves that in the most awesome of difficulties His children's faith waxes strongest.

11. 1 Peter 5:10

Suffering and human inadequacies bring maturity, stability and truth of God's Word.

12. 1 Peter 5:5,6

God must come against our pride. Humility, though, causes Him to bestow supernatural enablement for daily living.

13. Psalm 90:15-17

Life's troubles allow the beauty of the Lord to flow through our lives.

14. Psalm 75:6

Promotion comes from the Lord.

15. II Corinthians 4:9-21

Life's pressures can actually cause a furtherance of Christ's work.

16. II Corinthians 13:3-4

Christ's life is our proof of victory over human weaknesses.

17. Galatians 2:20

As a believer, Christ lives in me. Therefore I need to daily depend upon His divine strength.

18. Colossians 1: 10, 11

His power is sufficient to sustain the obedient believer in all circumstances.

19. John 15:5-7

Depending minute by minute upon the Lord brings miraculous results to the believer's life.

20. II Corinthians 12:9

When we are weak in our energies, His strength is able supernaturally to enable us.

Let's Get Personal !

1. Why does God allow us to come to the end of ourselves?

2. List some biblical characters that exemplify the quality of humility.

3. At what time in your life have you seen God resist your good works done in pride?

"LORD, ARE YOU TRYING TO TELL ME SOMETHING?! LIKE MAYBE I NEED TO BE HEADING A DIFFERENT DIRECTION?
SECURITY
INVESTMENTS
CAREER
SAVINGS

Chapter Three

Those Annoying Circumstances

By the way, things weren't all bad! There were some much needed and welcomed calms between the storms. I had just experienced one very exciting and fulfilling year assisting Tel-Evangelism International, a unique telephone outreach ministry as it expanded throughout our nation. We had joined a country church near our home and enjoyed the challenge of teaching a young adult Sunday school class and directing the church's community outreach program.

It may be that I just got my directions from the Lord mixed up. For months I had experienced an impression that the Lord was about to lead me into a new and much needed ministry. What was about to happen in my life later reminded me of my last high school football game. I was the quarterback and punter of the team and we were playing a highly rated school. Films of my game performance were to be sent to an out-of-state college for evaluation of my potential as a college player.

We were playing an exceptional game and holding the heavily favored opponent scoreless when the most bizarre event of my career occurred. It was fourth down and I was to punt the ball to the other team. A thirty mile-an-hour Florida breeze was blowing in the direction the ball was to be kicked and it should have sailed well down the field. Hoping to take advantage of that gusting wind, I tried to kick the ball as high as possible. The problem was, I kicked it too high...straight above my head to be exact! And you'll never guess what happened next. I kicked it too high with no downfield trajectory. It came straight down! You wouldn't want to venture at whose feet it landed, would you? Mine, of course. Then what? A punt for minus ten yards! Was I ever embarrassed!

What an unfortunate circumstance! A tough break. A bad bounce. After all, that's what life is all about, isn't it - good breaks, bad breaks, fortunate circumstances and unfortunate circumstances?

Really, now! Can we treat life so haphazardly? Does it all boil down to being at the right place at the right time with the right words to say? Can we "nutshell" our travels here on this earth into the feeble outlook that success comes to those who have either "the brains, the brawn, the bucks or the breaks"? Though I would have been too proud to admit it then, that is precisely how I operated for many years as a Christian.

I had often quoted Romans 8:28, "And we know that God causes all things to work together for good to those who love God, to those who are called according to His purpose".

Extraordinary afflictions
are not always the punishment
of extraordinary sins,
but sometimes the trial
of extraordinary graces.

God has many
sharp-cutting instruments,
and rough files for the polishing
of His jewels;
and those He especially loves,
and means to make
the most resplendent,
He tools upon the most.

Archbishop Leighton

I am positive that I never fully comprehended or practiced the vital truth contained in that scripture. For certainly, I reasoned, if a man works diligently enough at whatever he endeavors, learns from the mistakes he makes and does not have too many unfortunate circumstances: He will succeed?

The Dale who thought that way was once again to undergo a "baptism of reality." Out I launched into another ministry. This time doing something at which I had already proven myself to be competent: starting things from ground floor level. I would be assisting young pastors in the founding of new churches as well as teaching a seminar entitled (I do chuckle at this now!), *Christian Success Institute.*

I had the blessing of my home church, a board of director/ supporters and a bundle of ideas and energy. So I dove in. Researching areas that needed new churches, working with prospective pastors, speaking in churches and teaching the seminar. I was on top of the world! And, it would have seemed, on top of my circumstances.

"How difficult it is for us to see His hand when the 'whole world' has caved in around us."

Two very essential ingredients of those good circumstances were about to be reversed however. One was my health (which I will address later) and the other was our support. The board of supporters were happy with the work but were busily involved with churches and businesses of their own. They didn't mind spending what monies had already been raised, but it was Dale and not the board who was to raise all future monies. And let me assure you that getting a brand new ministry solidly supported is no overnight task - especially if you are finding yourself awakening every morning feeling as if you were just beat to a pulp in a prize fight!

To make matters more exasperating, no imaginable solution had appeared on the horizon. In time, the board chose to curtail its active involvement in the programs. With the ex-board and the ex-good health went the ex-ministry. With the ex-ministry went the income. The circumstances had indeed taken a turn for the worse. I now look back at this time and clearly see that God was masterfully at work in my life. But, oh, how difficult it is for us to see His hand when the whole world is caving in around us!

Speaking of circumstances, just what are those often annoying twists of fate, anyhow? Let's divide them into a few basic categories and see how God illustrates them - and what we might learn in the person of some of the Bible's most interesting characters:

GOD-BROUGHT CIRCUMSTANCES

The Patriarch Joseph has a most unique story to share with us today. Joseph, you will remember, was the teenager whose uncontrollably jealous brothers sold him into slavery to a group of wandering nomads. No sooner had he established himself as an upright and dependable "slave" than he was falsely accused of a grave offense, thrown into prison and there forgotten.

You will remember, too, that God had that same Joseph miraculously released from prison and thrust into the position of vice-pharaoh over the mighty land of Egypt.

You may shrink back
from the fierce storm of trial
. . . but go in!
God is there to meet you
in the center of all your trials,
and to whisper
to you secrets
which will make you
come forth
with a shining face
and an indomitable faith
that all the demons of Hell
shall never afterwards
cause to waiver.

E. A. Kilbourne

Be reminded, though, that this series of events was no overnight drama. As many as nineteen long years had elapsed as those roller coaster events transpired.

Joseph's own brothers, not recognizing him after many years of separation, came from their country to Egypt to buy food. After an emotionally-filled time of forgiveness and joyful re-union, Joseph made this remarkable statement to his awe-struck brothers, "You intended to harm me, but God intended it for good to accomplish what is now being done, the saving of many lives." (Genesis 50:20)

If anybody ever had the right to lie down and pound the floor in utter despondency and despair at his most unfortunate circumstances, Joseph did. But Joseph had the perception, even as a young man, to see well beyond those predicaments we call circumstances. Believing that his all-powerful God was in control of his life - though the future more than once looked absolutely hopeless - Joseph was careful to keep a pure, faith-filled heart before the Lord during those trying times.

We also have numerous opportunities to respond to life's very unpredictable circumstances. We may choose to lash out in resentment and bitter reaction toward them. Or we may choose to allow these twists of fate to cause us to draw closer to our Lord - while hurting, though not understanding, we feel we don't deserve what has befallen us.

The Author and Finisher of our faith will ultimately make something very beautiful out of something now very uncomely!

"Not only so, but we also rejoice in our sufferings, because we know that suffering produces perseverance; perseverance, character, and character, hope. And hope does not disappoint us, because God has poured out his love into our hearts by the Holy Spirit, whom He has given us." (Romans 5:3-5)

SATAN-BROUGHT CIRCUMSTANCES

Job had been minding his own business. Or, might we say, minding the Lord's business - worshipping the Lord, serving the Lord and sacrificing unto the Lord even in his children's behalf. Satan was just as sure as he could be that if things weren't going so good for Job that Job would not only sin but would even go so far as to blame the whole mess on the Lord.

And the old devil got an immediate opportunity to find out just what Job was made of spiritually. "The Lord said to Satan, 'Very well, then, he is in your hands; but you must spare his life.'" Did Satan ever go to town on that one! He took away Job's children, home and possessions. Not even his wife's respect was spared. Satan afflicted Job's body from head to toe with one of the most horrible of ailments: boils. Circumstantially, Job's whole world had become one nightmarish catastrophe.

Job, like Joseph, seemed to have ample reason to shake his fist at God for allowing these horrible circumstances. Yet, remarkably, God recorded this for us today. In all this, Job did not sin by charging God with wrongdoing. Job was hurting: physically, mentally and emotionally, but he remained faithful!

"I CAN'T SAY THIS MAKES SENSE TO ME AT ALL, LORD, AND I SURE DO HURT... BUT I WANT YOU TO KNOW THAT I TRUST YOU!"

The beautiful side of the picture though, is that Job did not lapse into circumstance-prompted despair. He responded God-ward! This is not true of vast multitudes of Christians today. For in the lives of Christians in most every city, town and village on the face of our globe you would find the sad example of Christians defeated and wrapped in needless despondency and depression because of Satan-brought circumstances.

I'm convinced that we believers have scarcely begun to understand the awesome spiritual warfare in which we are engaged while here on earth! In eternity we will be shocked - shocked not only at the phenomenal influence, massive organization and detailed scheming of the Wicked One, but amazed even more at the tools and powers that were available to us to resist the onslaught of the treacherous Deceiver. (John 14:11-31)

The fiery circumstantial darts of the devil and his forces are being hurled our way daily. Our response to these powerful attacks is so very crucial. Shall we attempt to dodge them, change their course or simply ignore them? Or shall we stand firm in Christ?

Job was genuinely humbled before the Lord and brought to an intimately closer companionship with Him as a result of the circumstances God allowed Satan to bring his way. So, too, can Satan-induced calamities become God's divine opportunities to bestow upon us the blessings and "joy unspeakable" which comes as we draw close to Him. Job's life was blessedly enriched spiritually, emotionally, mentally and even materially by his faith toward God. The same kind of divinely given benefits are awaiting our enjoyment.

> "Submit, yourselves, then, to God.
> Resist the devil, and he will flee from you.
> Come near to God and he will come near to you. Wash your hands, you sinners,
> and purify your hearts, you double-minded."
>
> **James 4:7**

Job's testing moved him from a man of great obedience to a man of much grace. We too may undergo this same reality today by looking heavenward for deliverance and strength from the snares of the Wicked One. But He gives us more grace. That is why Scripture says: God opposes the proud but gives grace to the humble. Humble yourselves before the Lord, and He will lift you up.

LIFE BROUGHT CIRCUMSTANCES

An amazing series of events occurred in the life of a remarkably patient patriarch named Isaac. It seems that Isaac's father, Abraham, had dug several much needed wells to supply water to his many servants and vast herds of animals. Years later Isaac returned to the area and redug those once bountiful water sources.

The local herdsmen were extremely jealous of Isaac's evident success at finding precious water. They hotly insisted that he vacate the very place where his men had so diligently labored to locate one of life's essential elements. Rather than dispute his "rights" and fight for his "possessions" Isaac mobilized his massive caravan and quietly moved on. Again, he dug. Again water was found. And, once again, the neighboring herdsmen rudely demanded him to move on. Surprisingly, Isaac did just that.

Now I don't know how you would have felt to see those priceless water sources so utterly abandoned. I think I would have certainly contemplated some "righteous" ground for all-out retaliation. Not so with Isaac. Though he obviously had the right to the very wells that his father had first dug, Isaac refused to allow those trying circumstances to cause him to lash out in bitter reaction. Instead, he committed the entire matter to his resourceful Lord.

Next, we see some unusual events unfold. Scripture tells us that not only did he tirelessly dig yet a third well but the "locals" started trembling in their sandals at his successes. Meanwhile, Abimelech had come to him from Gerar, with Ahuzzath, his personal adviser and Phicol, the commander of his forces. Isaac asked them, "Why have you come to me, since you were hostile to me and sent me away?" They answered, "We saw clearly that the Lord was with you; so we said, 'There ought to be a sworn agreement between us and you. Let us make a treaty with you that you will do us no harm, just as we did not molest you but always treated you well and sent you away in peace. And now you are blessed by the Lord.'" (Genesis 26:26-29) Isn't this phenomenal human rationalizing?

Isaac's deserted wells remind us of our own lives. There are those times when it seems that everything we attempt goes wrong. Or, when at long last we do succeed, some bizarre series of events swiftly nullifies all that rewarding accomplishment. Meanwhile, the guy-next-door or the can't-fail-relative or the fellow-Christian-at-work seems to have everything in life moving along as planned. Life is so very unpredictable and often so very frightening.

How vividly I recall the evening I sat with a young couple agonizing over the unexplainable loss of their beautiful child. A pat answer? The perfect words of comfort? The appropriate cliché? I could only tell them that God loved that child and that He loved them; that in reality there was no explanation. All we could do is that which a suffering Job did: trust Him.

> "Though He slay me, yet will I hope in Him;
> I will surely defend my ways to his face."
>
> **Job 13:15**

You've heard it said that "life is no respecter of persons." After all, Christians experience the same unexpected and fearfully unexplainable tragedies as do the most vile of sinners. And, yes, there will be times when there is no answer, no immediate logical explanation for the circumstances befalling us.

We must learn, as Isaac had learned; "to cast our innermost cares upon Him, knowing that He cares for us." (1 Pet 5:7)

We must learn to move on to yet another well, to know that God is pleased with the patient growth these would-be devastations are instilling in our lives. We must allow God to use these "life-brought" circumstances to teach us to walk by faith and not by sight, "And without faith it is impossible to please God" (Hebrews 11:6).

And tougher medicine still: "For it is commendable if a man bears up under the pain of unjust suffering because he is conscious of God. But how is it to your credit if you receive a beating for doing wrong and endure it? But if you suffer for doing good and you endure it, this is commendable before God." (1 Peter 2:19-20)

SELF-INFLICTED CIRCUMSTANCES

One would think that while churning around in the great fish's belly Jonah would surely have had a sincere change of heart about his resistance to God's instructions. The circumstances he had gotten himself into obviously dictated rethinking!

Out of that frightening form of transportation Jonah was ushered right in the direction of - you guessed it - Nineveh, that wicked city to which God had asked him to minister. With little other choice and with an evident reluctance, Jonah preached the Word of the Lord to these hopeless people. Miraculously, the whole city repented and was spared from what would have been total annihilation.

And of all imaginable reactions, Jonah was angry at God for sparing such ruthless sinners. So, what did he do next? He lapsed into a fit of depression!

And yet another circumstance was to flavor his self-inflicted misery: God miraculously grew a great gourd to shade Jonah from the intense heat as he wallowed in self-pity. An important lesson was in the making, though. "But at dawn the next day God provided a worm, which chewed the view so that it (the vine) withered. When the sun rose, God provided a scorching wind, and the sun blazed on Jonah's head so that he grew faint.

IF I CAN JUST GET OUT OF THIS ONE BIG JAM, MAYBE I CAN TALK TO THE LORD ABOUT SENDING A MORE QUALIFIED EVANGELIST TO NINEVAH!!!

“But God said to Jonah, ‘Do you have a right to be angry about the vine?’ ‘I do,’ he (Jonah) said. ‘I am angry enough to die.’ But the Lord said, ‘You have been concerned about this vine, though you did not tend it or make it grow. It sprang up overnight and died overnight. But Nineveh has more than a hundred and twenty thousand people who cannot tell their right hand from their left, and many cattle as well. Should I not be concerned about that great city?’ ” (Jonah 4:7-11)

Now, it is quite evident that Jonah had really dug himself into a hole by way of an extremely disobedient and thankless spirit! The real problem was, that rather than responding to God's promptings evidenced by these remarkable circumstances, Jonah kept on digging! He could have responded positively to his circumstances, searched his heart for sinful, unforgiving attitudes and asked for God's cleansing. What strength and victory could have come his way! But he did not. Nor did the children of Korah. Nor did Achan. Nor did Eli’s sons. Nor did Saul. Nor did Absalom. Nor did numerous of Israel’s and Judah's kings. Nor did Judas Iscariot. Nor did multitudes of God's needlessly miserable children down through the ages!

“Nor did I!” Will that be the epitaph on our gravestones? Life could have been an absolute blessed experience. Far better than I could have asked for or even imagined. But I chose to hold on to my goals. My ambitions. My way of thinking. My desires. My life. I chose to spend a lifetime stubbornly attempting to alter or ignore life’s annoying circumstances. I chose to obey my inward desires and impulses rather than to respond, as a willing child to the circumstance-brought redirections of my loving Lord.

Let it never be said, however, that it could not have been

different. Let it never be said that the strength and the wisdom and the courage available through God's Holy Spirit dwelling within me was inadequate. He had more than adequate solutions for the trials and the testings and the hurts and the failures I experienced in this life. God's infallible Word is simply packed full of accounts of two kinds of people who have managed to work themselves into dire circumstances. There are the Samsons, Solomons and Jonahs whose self-willed resistance to life's circumstances literally ran over them. And, there are the Abrahams, the Jacobs, the Davids, the Hezekiahs and the Peters who - though suffering the often severe consequences of their impetuousness - looked to God for supernatural guidance and redirected their lives accordingly!

The key then in this matter of circumstances, is not so much trying to reason out all the whys of our predicament or to wallow in the guilt that might come from knowing why. The key is an increasing faith in the face of life's unpredictable predicaments! It is learning to lean on Him even when our emotions are insisting on a human reason or an immediate way out. It is a minute-by-minute learning to trust process.

> "I know what it is to be in need, and I know what it is to have plenty. I have learned the secret of being content in any and every situation, whether well fed or hungry, whether living in plenty or in want. I can do everything through him who gives me strength."
>
> **Philippians 4:12**

CHAPTER THREE
Verse Summaries

1. Genesis 50:20
   God used even man's evil intents to achieve ultimate good for him.

2. Romans 5:3-5
   Life's trials bring patience which leads to spiritual maturity.

3. Psalm 118:5-6
   We are not to fear the evil intentions of fellow men.

4. John 16:33
   He who indwells us has overcome the evils of this world.

5. II Corinthians 4:7-18
   The trials and struggles of this life are superseded by the hope of that which is to come.

6. Job 2:6
   Satan may assault Job, but must spare his life.

7. Job 2:7, 8
   Job is gravely afflicted by Satan.

8. Job 1:22
   In the face of tremendous pressures, Job does not sin.

9. John 14:11-31
Christ promises comfort and power to His followers.

10. James 4:7, 8
Instruction on effectively resisting Satan.

11. James 4:6
Humility brings divine enablement.

12. Genesis 26:26-29 -
A vivid illustration of the believer's opportunity to respond to God even in the most ridiculous of life's predicaments.

13. Job 13:15
Job's commitment to trust God no matter what the extent of his circumstances.

14. I Peter 5:7
We can trust God with our every problem because of His supreme love for us.

15. I Peter 2:19-20
Learning to patiently endure heartache you did not bring on yourself pleases God.

16. Philippians 1:12
The pressures in Paul's life were an instrument of God in furthering the cause of Christ.

17. Psalms 16-17
Setting our spiritual eyesight upon Him produces supernatural strength and peace.

18. Philippians 1:27-30
    This life's pressures are not to discourage us but to know the depths of "Christ-in-us".

19. Jonah 4:7-11
    Jonah's despondency at the Lord's sparing of Ninevah.

20. Numbers 16
    God's response to the disobedience of the children of Korah.

21. Joshua 7
    Achan suffers the grave consequences of deceit.

22. I Samuel 2-4
    Eli's sons suffer consequences of violating the priestly office.

23. I Samuel 13-15
    A fearful Saul takes God's matters into his own hands.

24. II Samuel 13-19
    David's son, Absalom, attempts to overthrow his father's kingdom.

25. I & II Kings
    A history of the tragic lives of many of Israel's and Judah's kings.

26. Matthew 26

Judas allows Satan to prompt his betrayal of Christ.

27. Philippians 4:12, 13

Learning contentment in all things is a key to God's power being released in our lives.

28. Philippians 1:6

God's assurance that He will, in His divine persistence, work diligently to bring every child of His to spiritual maturity.

29. Romans 8:37-39

We can truly be more than conquerors over the problems and circumstances of this life because of His powerful love for us.

Let's Get Personal !

1. List the four kinds of circumstances the author uses to describe the human dilemma.

2. List one personal example for each of the above:

a.

b.

c.

d.

3. What scripture would you use to affirm God's supernatural peace in the midst of difficult circumstances?

My God,
I have never thanked Thee
for my thorn.
I have thanked Thee
a thousand times
for my roses,
but not once for my thorn . . .
Teach me the glory
of my cross;
teach me the value
of my thorn.
Show me that I have
climbed to Thee
by the path of pain.
Show me that my tears
have made my rainbows.

George Matheson

Chapter Four

The Beauty of Suffering

I had just returned from extensive testing by Dr. Charles Harrison, an Atlanta Falcon football team physician and one of the finest internists in Atlanta. The results were not as I had expected. Three days of almost every conceivable test found nothing amiss. Absolutely nothing! When you are the kind of person who never seems to run out of energy or ideas, feeling as "rock-bottom" awful as I felt was absolutely exasperating. And this was to be no overnight inconvenience. In fact, the emotional upheaval I experienced during the two years that I was engulfed by a mysterious illness is difficult to put into words, even these many years later.

There was certainly not the faintest question in my mind that something was absolutely wrong inside of me. I couldn't sleep. I had zero energy. Every bone in my body ached. How vividly I remember those days that I literally crawled to the supper table, only to stare at the food my body refused to eat. I felt like and looked like I was only half-alive! I had even lost my optimism. And that alone left me wondering if I was not being slowly ushered out of this life. What a chain reaction that infirmity was to cause. Income, career, purpose in life and even the will to live, all but vanished.

There were some things that I did have, though. Things even more important than career or security. I had a very special opportunity to grow through suffering. I had a wonderful Savior and Friend who was soon to reveal a far greater dimension of His love to myself and Rachel. I had a miraculously healthy, growing little Julia and a beautiful new addition, Natalie. The little country church we attended in the northern suburbs of Atlanta was a special blessing. It was a church whose people genuinely cared about us and ministered to us in both spiritual and material ways. And, though we struggled with anger and bitterness in our marriage relationship, we both had an overwhelming desire to know and to obey God.

> "Only after the Lord brought us to a far deeper spiritual alertness did the sunlight begin to glimmer through the dark clouds."

Rachel was the third of six children of a missionary family. Not knowing what earthly source God would use to provide the next meal was no new experience to her. But neither of us were prepared for the absolute helplessness this infirmity had brought into almost every phase of our daily existence. There were countless times when we questioned, "Will Dale ever be well again? Will we ever again have a ministry? What are we to do with all of these bills? How will they be paid?"

How quickly we discovered that it is one thing to talk about unwavering faith in difficult situations - while it's a whole new ballgame to put that concept into practice when surrounded by such dismal conditions.

What in the world was happening? What did we do to deserve this? Is God angry at us? The questions just kept coming and coming. And to make matters more perplexing, the answers did not come with the questions . . at least not for what seemed like an eternity of month after month after month.

Why does God allow infirmity in the life of a Christian? Is sickness nothing more than a necessary evil we must all endure while we are pilgrims on this sin-filled planet? Does God have some definite purpose to accomplish through infirmity? How important it is that we understand the purpose of suffering. Surely, nothing will get someone studying the scriptures, meditating, and talking to God more than going through a little of the fire. That's where I was!

As His Word promises, God provided us the strength and encouragement we needed to go through this special and difficult time in our lives - not just one day at a time but literally one moment at a time! And, ultimately, He would wondrously provide "a way of escape." Only after the Lord had brought us to a far deeper spiritual alertness, did the sunlight begin to glimmer through the dark clouds.

During two difficult but blessed years, God graciously revealed to me wonderful insights on suffering.

FROM HURRICANES TO RAINBOWS

Growing up in a home facing the Atlantic Ocean was not without adventure, especially during Hurricane season. How vividly I remember going through three of those giant storms - two of which were simply devastating. Once our home was completely washed away, and on two later occasions, the lower level of a different home was all but totally swept clean by the fury of the wind and the waves.

It was astonishing to learn later that winds were recorded at two hundred twelve miles per hour during Hurricane Donna. The damage left in the wake of that terrible storm was almost unbelievable. Jagged pilings from washed-away bridges evidenced Donna's vicious attack. Thousands of homes literally vanished. The frightening high tides and mammoth waves washed ashore and literally deposited an ocean-going ship right in our neighbor's front yard!

The stench from the flames of food stores and restaurants being burnt to prevent food contamination was a bleak reminder of the number of life long businesses that were forever lost. Hundreds of boats representing a fisherman's lifetime of savings, had sunk to the bottom of the ocean or bay. What little was left of one's possessions was likely to be stolen by the hundreds of looters who swarmed the defenseless Keys. Aerial photographs indeed gave the appearance of a giant fork having ruthlessly raked the tiny chain of islands of virtually every iota of its magnificence.

There was a breathtakingly beautiful rainbow to be seen after Hurricane Donna's violence had subsided. But it went almost unnoticed. Without roads or bridges or homes or fresh water or food it was somewhat difficult to focus upon rainbows. In fact, few of us really believed the once beautiful Keys would ever be the same again.

Five amazing years had passed since Donna when Hurricane Betsy approached. In those five years what had seemed impossible had happened. Bridges had been replaced. Homes had been rebuilt. New boats had been purchased. New trees had been replanted. A special channel had been dredged into the deep water to remove the ship out of our neighbor's yard.

Hurricane Betsy was quite oblivious to all of these hundreds of thousands of tear-filled hours of clean-up and rebuilding. Her fury struck us squarely in the face and the damages were much the same as before. Another rainbow appeared and again we were too awestruck to give it so much as a glance. As if that wasn't enough, another destructive storm struck just two years later. With each time of loss and suffering came an increased strength. An extra bit of courage. An unexplainable hope. A renewed appreciation for life itself. As time passes, the wounds of suffering do begin to heal.

Largely gone from the memories of the victims is the acuteness of the heartache experienced in the aftermath of those storms' terrible destruction. For in time - and, indeed, what may seem to be an eternity - life's rainbows do some. Life's stormy experiences of suffering and loss do pass on. The sunshine of hope does again glow brightly. And through each painful upheaval God has been instilling rainbow like beauty of character in our lives. Though the storm has been painful, the rebuilding has fashioned firmer foundations. Praise His Name!

AFFLICTIONS THAT REDIRECT PRIORITIES

Here is an overview of how God uses different aspects of suffering (and the attidues of failure and defeat which often accompany that suffering) to build specific character qualities into the lives of His children.

Remember our impetuous apostle friend, Peter. What mental and emotional anguish (afflictions) he experienced after three times denying his Lord!

His hopes that the Messiah would set up an immediate earthly kingdom were shattered. His ambitions to stick by his Master in the face of any and all opposition had been crushed. And more was yet to come! For in His infinite wisdom the Lord knew that Peter still had some of his hopes fixed upon the tangible things of this world.

In other words, Christ was telling Peter he needed to change his priorities. He needed to look directly to the Lord for his answers instead of failing back on human intellect. Our Lord desires that very same thing in your life and my life today. He is gradually souring the mental tastes of our earth-life so that our heavenly appetite might be enlarged.

May life's afflictions prompt us to look to Him to instill within us - through His Word, His spirit and His doings - a burning desire to make Him the priority in every area of our lives. "By faith Moses, when he had grown up, refused to be known as the son of Pharoah's daughter. He chose to be mistreated along with the people of God rather than to enjoy the pleasures of sin for a short time. He regarded disgrace for the sake of Christ as of greater value than the treasures of Egypt, because he was looking ahead to his reward." (Hebrews 11:24-26)

I can still believe
that a day comes for all of us,
however far off it may be,
when we shall understand;
when these tragedies
that now blacken and darken
the very air of heaven for us
will sink into their places
in a scheme so august,
so magnificent,
so joyful, that we shall laugh
for wonder and delight.

Arthur Christopher Benson

Likening milk to the spiritual food of immature Christians, the inspired writer exhorts the Hebrew Christians to redirect their priorities by learning to concentrate on things of eternal value.

> Anyone who lives on milk, being still an infant,
> is not acquainted
> with the teaching about righteousness.
> But solid food is for the mature,
> who by constant use have trained themselves
> to distinguish good from evil.
>
> **Hebrews 5:13,14**

PERSECUTION THAT BUILDS HEAVENLY HOPE

Perhaps one of our greatest problems here in America is that we understand so little about persecution and the blessed spiritual victories it can be instrumental in bringing. God's promise is that "all who live a godly life will experience a certain amount of persecution." (2 Timothy 3:12) often coming from places we might least expect: our home, our school, our job, our spiritually-blinded friends or relatives.

The key issue, though, is not the source of the persecution we may be receiving but rather the quality of life that persecution is prompting in us. Persecution, be it great or small, should not provoke us to give up and retreat from society but to affix our hope - the very core of our inner motivations - on things eternal. Correctly responding to persecution means we will begin thinking like and disciplining our lives so that those earthly ambitions are replaced by heavenly hope. "Blessed are you when people insult you, persecute you, and falsely say all kinds of evil against you because of me. Rejoice and be glad, because great is your reward in heaven, for in the same way they persecuted the prophets who were before you." (James 4:6)

INFIRMITY THAT BRINGS LOVE

Just as I was graduating from college I was stunned by the results of some extensive hospital testing. My kidneys were afflicted with the same degenerative disease that took my mother's life while she was still in her prime. What thoughts and emotions chilled my spine. Every day of my life would, in some way, be afflicted by this unyielding disease.

Loss of energy, trips to the emergency room, the label of "uninsurable" and complex family scenarios would often drain my emotions and cloud the future.

Even now, as I am approaching kidney failure (I write the word "failure" believing that at any instant God may "re-create" those failing kidneys) I can assure you that "His grace is sufficient." I can attest to the fact that His strength seems to get stronger as we get weaker. And you know what else? Most of the sthings and accomplishments of this life aren't very high up life's totem pole in comparison to good health. And one of the really good things about uncertain health as I see it - is that it's quite a bit easier to be bold in one's witness for Christ. Since none of us are permanent in this life, we have nothing to lose and everything to gain in being bold for Christ's kingdom.

The Apostle Paul knew when sickness or impairment or even

physical problems caused directly by Satan and his emissaries came upon him, drastically limiting his own strengths and energies, that a wonderful strength from within would then "kick into high gear."

Yes, infirmity has a special place in the growing process for us Christians. Some will experience it often. Some will seldom be within its grip. A few will pass through this life virtually free from its tenacious grasp. But when we are experiencing some form of it, let us not forget that Christ himself fully comprehends every iota of pain we are experiencing.

"Therefore, since we have a great high priest who has gone through the heavens, Jesus the Son of God, let us hold firmly to the faith we profess. For we do not have a high priest who is unable to sympathize with our weaknesses, but we have one who has been tempted in every way, just as we are - yet was without sin. Let us then approach the throne of grace with confidence, so that we may receive mercy and find grace to help us in our time of need."

We need grace to help us thank God even for the pain; grace to help us to a point of utter dependence upon the strength and comforting power of the indwelling Holy Spirit; grace to help develop in us a divine tenderness - a love that is supernatural. That is the kind of love that simply draw people to Him - whether they be believers who have backslidden from intimate fellowship with Him, or non-Christians who may resist the drawing power of His agape love.

PLEASE STOP PRAYING

An old friend of mine shared this story of a young man who came to him and asked, "Doctor, I want the kind of relationahip with Christ that you have." The good doctor asked that they get on their knees and pray. His prayer, "Oh God, give this young man problems and heartaches and disappointment. Give him great trials and infirmity. Give him . . ." "Wait, wait, wait. Please doctor. Please stop praying!" pleaded the trembling young man. "I thought you wanted a consecrated life" was the doctor's reply. "Without trials and testing you will never experience the kind of life you are looking for." "Oh," gasped the wide eyed young believer, "I guess I'd better give this a little more thought."

The bottom line is this: when infirmity saps the life out of us, we quickly get back to the basics. And nothing is more powerful than the basics of agape love.

"Love is patient, love is kind. It does not envy, it does not boast, it is not proud. It is not rude, it is not self-seeking, it is not easily angered, it keeps no record of wrongs. Love does not delight in evil but rejoices with the truth. It always trusts, always hopes, always perseveres." (I Corinthians 13:4-8)

TEMPTATION THAT BUILDS FAITH

Daniel and his three companions, Shadrak, Meshak and Abednego had their share of temptation! They were first told that a simple bowing down and worshipping of a golden image - even if that image was not believed to be a god - would keep them out of a fiery furnace. Later, Daniel was informed that a refraining from public prayer would keep him from being cast into a den of ravenous lions. And you know the rest of the story!

But the interesting part of that event is what happened in those young men's lives. Just think what it would do to you to be thrown into an intensely blazing furnace, fellowship with an angel or perhaps the Lord Himself while in that furnace, and then be brought out without even the smell of smoke on your clothes. Or, to be thrown into a den of half-starved lions and have them lie gently at your feet. That would dramatically build your faith, would it not? And that is precisely what happened. Those already dedicated men became even more powerful in faithful service to their great God.

"An extreme example," you are thinking. "My faith would be strengthened, too, if I went through that kind of experience." First of all, don't rule out phenomenal faith-building experiences in today's life. Miracles are by no means extinct. Remember, too, that though you may never experience a temptation of such great magnitude, God does have a faith-building program custom-designed for you.

Those everyday temptations, those seemingly insignificant little testings, are not without divine purpose. Each additional day that God graciously gives will bring ample temptation - to sin, to compromise Biblical truth, to go opposite the Holy Spirit's leading, to do that which would gratify self rather than to meet the needs of others. Each of these temptations brings also a choice. An opportunity for us to draw upon His limitless reservoir of strength and to refuse the lure of our own selfish desires. To watch our heavenly Father do His part in giving us ". . grace to help us in our time of need." (Hebrews 4:16) "To strengthen our faith by His mighty uplifting hand." (Isaiah 41:10)

How vividly I remember, after months of lying helplessly on my back and wondering if life would ever again be "unscrambled," the message God communicated to me. I was reading His Word - but getting very little out of it - when this unmistakable divine thought was given me, "Dale, stop worrying about your ministries, your success and your future and start cultivating an intimate, special relationship with me - for I am more interested in what you become than in what you accomplish." And, how exciting it became as the more I focused upon Him the less power my infirmity seemed to have over my body!

Infirmity. Affliction. Temptation. Persecution. We would all be glad to do without any of them! But they are going to come - and with them will also come the uniquely wonderful opportunity for genuine spiritual growth. The next time we are swamped by one of life's dark and dreadful and seemingly endless storms, let us remember that the tempest will pass. The forces and pressures and hurts of that onslaught are the very ingredients needed to produce a breathtaking spiritual rainbow. To make a positive, faith-building adventure out of even the ugliest and most hopeless of life's painful experiences is dependent upon God's grace.

> My grace is sufficient for you,
> for my power is made perfect in weakness.
> Therefore I will boast
> all the more gladly about my weaknesses,
> so that Christ's power may rest on me."
>
> **2 Corinthians 12:9**

CHAPTER FOUR
Scriptural Insightss

1. John 1:16
   Through Christ we receive grace heaped upon grace.

2. 2 Corinthians 4:15-18
   Our Lord's supernatural strength helps us through even lifes most extreme circumstances.

3. 1 Peter 5:10
   Response to tribulation allows God's abundant grace to strengthen and mature His children.

4. Job 23:10
   Job's commitment to the Lord - even in severe testing - promises to bring blessing and reward.

5. Psalm 30:5
   God's promise of joy even during a time of great struggle.

6. 2 Corinthians 1:3
   The believer is assured mercy and limitless comfort.

7. John 21:22
   Peter is rebuked for concerning himself himself with some one else's future.

8. Hebrews 11:24-26
   Moses refuses earthly attainment in favor of spiritual riches.

9. Hebrews 5:13,14
   Our maturity as a Christian is measured by our digesting and applying the depth of God's Word.

10. 2 Timothy 3:12
    In the last days (and certainly not in the last days only) persecution is to come upon the righteous Christian.

11. Matthew 5:11,12
Persecution can cause the Christian to rejoice.

12. Psalm 56.3
When apparent reason to fear comes, commit your soul unreservedly to Him.

13. 1 Corinthians 4:9-15
Persecution is not reason for shame but is to be accepted as a part of bearing one's cross.

14. 2 Thessalonians 1:3-6
Patiently and faithfully enduring suffering makes one better fit for God's kingdom.

15. 2 Corinthians 12:9
Paul does not despise physical infirmity, knowing that Christ works mightily even through a frail human vessel.

16. Hebrews 4:14-16
We may go unreservedly to the throne of grace for help and comfort knowing that Christ literally experienced the same kind of suffering.

17. 1 Corinthians 13:4-8
Love's behaviors and never failing qualities are listed.

18. Daniel 6:4-10
Daniel is tempted to compromise his commitment to the Lord in order to preserve his life.

My God,
I have never thanked Thee
for my thorn.
I have thanked Thee
a thousand times
for my roses,
but not once for my thorn . . .
Teach me the glory
of my cross;
teach me the value
of my thorn.
Show me that I have
climbed to Thee
by the path of pain.
Show me that my tears
have made my rainbows.

George Matheson

Let's Get Personal !

1. How can suffering be used of God to redirect the focus of our priorities?

2. List one verse of scripture about suffering that you would use to minister to someone else.

3. Describe one instance of persecution that you have experienced on behalf of your faith.

Someone has described
a modern American
as a person who drives
a bank-financed car
over a bond-financed highway
on credit card gas
to open a charge account
at a department store
so he can fill his savings
and loan financed home
with installment-purchased
furniture.
May this not also be
a description of many modern
professed Christians?

The Mystery of Prayer

Chapter Five

Dollars and Sense

Have you ever met an individual who could give the best advice in the world on a particular subject but simply could not make that same advice work for himself? This author is one such person when the subject is how to operate a successful business. How distinctly I recall the evening Rachel and I were at dinner with several other couples and I overheard her bragging about her husband to a friend. The conversation went something like this, "It seems like people just gravitate to Dale for business advice and he has genuinely helped several friends become very successful with his advice. The problem is: those good ideas never seem to work for Dale!"

Let me tell you about the madhouse of a summer that really put the icing on the cake of my business career. Looking back at it now, the whole ordeal was one amazing, hilarious event; quite nightmarish when it all occurred but very rich in spiritual lessons. Here is how the adventure unfolded.

Since my writing and public relations days in college I had wanted to own a printing and publishing company. My church planting and seminar ministries were just beginning to flourish and what better time to own a Christian printing company?

The added income would be used to cover the expense of supplying free brochures and gospel tracts to new churches. And, providing quality printing at economical prices for the many Christian businesses and ministries in Greater Atlanta would be an added ministry in itself. For over two years everything went as planned. The only real problem was my soft heart. I just hated to charge an extra dime when doing work for fellow Christians, many of whom were on limited budgets. Not consistently covering expenses has its distinct drawbacks though. And it only took one iceberg to sink the Titanic!

The iceberg for that little business surfaced in a rather peculiar manner. Late one spring afternoon the graphics director of a large Christian ministry called with a camouflaged time-bomb. He informed me that he had the perfect job for our small company and couldn't imagine why another printing company hadn't jumped on this one at the price he was able to pay! Though he was sincere in his intentions of giving us work, little did he know what an unconscionable education that project would bring!

As the job progressed, it became terrifyingly evident that thirty thousand multi-page directories was indeed not the perfect job for our small shop. No turning back now, though. We rented the facilities of a larger print shop, hired a dozen high school students for the summer, and set out to assemble more than a million pages into the thousands of directories.

The fun was just beginning! One of Atlanta's hottest summers had arrived. The teenagers were getting more irritable by the day. The equipment was constantly breaking down. There were five-foot-high stacks of paper all over the other printing company's shop. Could anything more go wrong? You guessed it! Dale and his sweaty, fussy helpers were evicted! Where to now? Where else but to the entire lower level of our house.

And to make matters in our humble abode even more interesting, a missionary family had already been staying with us for a number of months. Two families, twelve fussy helpers, one exasperated young businessman and one million pieces of paper. All stuffed into one topsy turvy house! Needless to say, the substantial financial losses incurred in that unforgettable job took a grave toll. The printing company had to be sold to recoup some of the loss. Three very long years later I paid the last of the four installment loans I was forced to secure.

What have I learned from this and two other similarly exasperating business ventures? For a starter, I have learned that I am to be in ministry and not in business! As a couple, Rachel and I have learned that our special spiritual endowments are to encourage, to teach, and to function administratively. We are to minister particularly within the range of those spiritual gifts. If God wants material profit to come our way then it is not to be through some brilliant scheme of ours but rather from a source unexplainably, undeniably from Him. We have learned that while my business counsel may continue to help others, we are to be content with whatever material benefits God gives us or decides not to give us.

"But I'm not called to the ministry," you are thinking. "I

can't afford to fail in business!" From a strictly human standpoint, you are right: you cannot afford to fail! If God knows that material failure will bring you ultimately to greater spiritual riches, however, you cannot afford not to fail! "And if I do fail, what do I do for grocery money in the meantime?" Good question. And there are answers. Let's take a look at what God may be doing in our lives through the provision of, or the distinct absence of, that elusive necessity we call money.

HEAVENWARD ATTENTION

What will more swiftly tilt our focus upward than an empty bank account? An unexpected depletion of money may often be God's way of getting both our attention and our interest directed toward Him. Might it be that the very scripture that we would hastily apply to the world's millionaires needs to be a little more carefully considered for us "average American Christians" today? "Command those who are rich in this present world not to be arrogant nor to put their hope in wealth, which is so uncertain, but to put their hope in God, who richly provides us with everything for our enjoyment." (1 Timothy 6:17)

Remember the prodigal son? As long as he had money in his pocket he didn't need the strength and security of his father. Aren't we often like that? As long as there is earthly security, heavenly dependence drifts quickly into the mystical "great somewhere". As we soothe ourselves with "isn't God wonderful" kinds of statements that are so easy to utter, we pay little actual attention to Him or to His "instruction manual".

Can we learn from the experience of that self-willed prodigal son? "After he had spent everything, there was a severe famine in that whole country, and he began to be in need. So he went and hired himself out to a citizen of that country, who sent him to his fields to feed pigs. He longed to fill his stomach with the pods that the pigs were eating, but no one gave him anything."

"When he came to his senses, he said, 'How many of my father's hired men have food to spare, and here I am starving to death! I will set out and go back to my father and say to him: Father, I have sinned against heaven and against you. I am no longer worthy to be called your son; make me like one of your hired men.' So he got up and went to his father. But while he was still a long way off, his father saw him and was filled with compassion for him; he ran to his son, threw his arms around him and kissed him." (Luke 15:14-20)

How vividly I recall a time in my life that I was scurrying about juggling the physical and financial pressures of three ministries. As these demands became unbearable, the Lord quite distinctly communicated this message to me: "Be still and know that I am God." (Psalm 46:10) Was the wind ever knocked out of me! Here I was "busy" serving the Lord, but my personal spiritual growth was going nowhere. God simply used financial pressure to get me to listen to that "still small voice". His message: the quality of spiritual life within ultimately determines the effectiveness of your ministry without!

A WONDERFUL OPPORTUNITY FOR INCREASED FAITH

Nowhere are the dynamics of faith better illustrated than in the lives of those remarkable first century believers. They were special messengers called to demonstrate an amazing spirit of willingness to share: "All the believers were one in heart and mind. No one claimed that any of his possessions was his own, but they shared everything they had. With great power the apostles continued to testify to the resurrection of the Lord Jesus, and much grace was upon them all." (Acts 4:32,33) An abstract story from scripture with little realistic application today? So the devil himself would have us think!

It seems, though, that few Christians today ever come to the point of divorcing themselves far enough from the deceitfulness of this world's riches to ever experience the reality of these words: “But godliness with contentment is great gain. For we brought nothing into the world, and we can take nothing out of it. But if we have food and clothing, we will be content with that.” (1 Timothy 6:6-8)

In other words, my focus may need changing. It may well be that I am operating too much by sight and far too little by faith. My primary pursuit in life may need redirecting - a renewed attention to spiritual growth as opposed to the subtle - but very real - obsession with material security or accumulation.

“Consider how the lilies grow. They do not labor or spin. Yet I tell you, not even Solomon in all his splendor was dressed like one of these. If that is how God clothes the grass of the field, which is here today, and tomorrow is thrown into the fire, how much more will he clothe you, O you of little faith! And do not set your heart on what you will eat or drink; do not worry about it. For the pagan world runs after all such things, and your Father knows that you need them. But seek His kingdom, and these things will be given to you as well.“ (Luke 12:27-31)

A NEW DIRECTION IN LIFE

What a picture of the importance of earthly stewardship - time, talents, and treasures - we see painted in the life of Moses. By slaying the Egyptian Moses was, in essence, attempting to launch his own career as the initiator of God's long-promised deliverance of Israel from the ruthless Egyptians. God had other plans though. For the career Moses was to fulfill required enormous patience and steadfastness. How did God instill these and other stabilizing qualities into Moses' life? Not as one might have expected! For not five, or ten or twenty or thirty, but for forty years Moses lived in the wilderness. Day after day in mundane repetition, he tended to the herds of his father-in-law, Jethro.

Those were not wasted years, though. For a remarkably patient and absolutely humble Moses then became God's human instrument in the monumental task of managing a million-plus indecisive Israelites. And that was no easy job! The "patience heaped upon patience" God had instilled in Moses was all dramatically put to the test as he led Israel out of Egypt, through forty years of journeying and to the threshold of the Promised Land.

Thus, we see that time or ability or material security is not nearly as important to God as the quality of life He desires to build in us. If a business or financial failure - or even several of them - is what is necessary to prompt us toward more Godly living and toward the wisdom to benefit from our mistakes, then praise be to His name!

You know what? God will never waste the failures He allows into our lives. (Luke 21:34) "That the God of our Lord Jesus Christ, the Father of glory, may give to you a spirit of wisdom and of revelation in the knowledge of Him. I pray that the eyes of your heart may be enlightened, so that you may know what is the hope of his calling, what are the riches of the glory of His inheritance in the saints." (Ephesians 1:17,18)

And what about our Promised Land? Will we ever "arrive"? Will we ever achieve any degree of material success in this life?

Do we today find ourselves in the wilderness, wandering and wondering what lies ahead? Has that which we felt was to be our life's work failed?

Has the "mat" of our financial goals been yanked out from under us more than once? Let us not be disheartened. For Moses' wilderness training is just one of the many examples in His Word that God has given us a source of assurance that He always knows what is best for each and every one of His children. God never, never, makes a mistake. He will see to it that every willing child of His is not only directed toward the right livelihood but given the tools of discipline to handle in a God-honoring manner the material benefits gleaned from that vocation. (Proverbs 16:19-20)

A STEP FURTHER

I don't know of a single Bible scholar who believes that Job lost his children, his home and all of his worldly possessions because he was in a spiritually disobedient condition. Nor do I know of one who believes that Job was not spiritually richer at the end of his amazing ordeal.

Precious metals - like precious Saints - are seldom purified apart from intense heat!

"But I'm growing spiritually. I sense an increasing knowledge of the Lord and I am committed to serving Him in every area of my life," you might plead. "Why would God allow any more financial failure to come my way?" Precious metals - as precious Saints - are seldom purified apart from intense heat!

"Dear friends, do not be surprised at the painful trial you are suffering, as though something strange were happening to you. But rejoice that you participate in the sufferings of Christ, so that you may be overjoyed when his glory is revealed." (1 Peter 4:12-13)

To the Christian, money can be likened to a spiritual thermometer. The problems we have because of it (or the lack of it!) are often a vivid indication of a deeper-rooted spiritual problem. The financial struggles and failures we experience may be specific warning signals from God. Once these warning signals capture our attention, God's Spirit can then begin to show us what problem, sin or needed change of direction He wants us to deal with.

We must always keep in mind this profound promise: "Whoever can be trusted with very little can also be trusted with much, and whoever is dishonest with much will not be trusted at all. So if you have not been trustworthy in handling worldly wealth, who will trust you with true riches? And if you have not been trustworthy with someone else's property, who will give you property of your own?" (Luke 16:10-12)

From the pastor's point of view, it has been fascinating - though sometimes heartbreaking - to view the changes in people as the years go by. I have often observed that it is an increase in material things (and the financial means, credit included, to acquire those things) that indicates the first stage of degenerating spiritual health. I have seen many families who were making great spiritual strides when they were suffering financially. Then came a little prosperity. The second job. The big break. The overtime and double overtime. And along with that taste of prosperity came an amazing revitalization of interest in material things and a gradual dulling of their spiritual senses.

For with that prosperity almost inevitably came a busier and more demanding schedule. No time now for regular daily personal or family Bible study. The pressure of time commitments did not permit consistent fellowship with fellow believers or regular attendance at discipleship-building meetings. Busy-ness had become a substitute for spirituality. With the sharpening of earthly senses, the love for believers and unbelievers fades; and, poof, that solid, growing church family is seen no more!

Is earthly prosperity wrong and sinful? No, and certainly not when one's spirituality is not negatively affected by it. Let us not forget, though, that our relentless enemy is ever scheming to bankrupt us spiritually. As the tireless god of this world, he loves nothing more than to see a subtle increasing love of money and material things gradually take the place of our spiritual commitments.

"It is often an increase in material things that indicates the first stage of degenerating spiritual health."

While we are sensing this divine guidance through the instrument of money, it is most important that we do not misread His navigation. We need to be certain that our financial situation is something more than impatience or greed or lack of reality. We must be assured that His divine hand is at work - be it supernaturally providing or withholding or simply putting us on hold. And there will never be a more accurate source of discerning His ways than through careful study of and meditation on His holy Word.

As a Christian
cannot experience
the fullness of the Holy Spirit
until he surrenders ownership
of his life to Christ,
so too, he cannot experience
peace in the area of finances
until he has surrendered
total control
of this area to God
and accepted his position
as a steward.

Larry Burkett

Before we plummet into despair about any monetary entanglement which we might be experiencing, let us consider these remarkable words, "Dear friend, I pray that you may enjoy good health and that all may go well with you, even as your soul is getting along well." (3 John 2)

God's design promises that there would be both earthly increase and physical well being as our spiritual being prospers. However, He does not always provide in the timing, manner, or magnitude we might humanly desire.

God always has our ultimate best at heart - even in those dilemmas which may come upon us momentarily. With that assurance, we can face each new day and each new problem with the knowledge that the financial trials which come our way are a unique opportunity for God to show Himself strong on our behalf.

CHAPTER FIVE
Verse Summaries

1. Philippians 3:11-19
   Though often not as we might expect, in His own creative way God does supply our needs.

2. Proverbs 27:23-27
   The importance of and rewards of diligence with one's material possessions.

3. I Timothy 6:17
   We are admonished to depend upon God, not material security.

4. Matthew 6:25 & 33 -
   As the spiritual values of life overwhelmingly outweigh the material, we must make seeking heavenly things a priority.

5. Job 1:21 -
   We can take no earthly thing with us upon leaving this world.

6. Luke 15:14-20 -
   A once-rebellious, now broken son returns to a forgiving father.

7. Acts 4:32-33
   The early church learns to share material possessions based upon each of the others' needs.

8. Genesis 3:1-5
Satan's tactics of temptation by "logic".

9. II Corinthians 11:3, 14
The god of this world stops at nothing to blind us from truth.

10. I Timothy 6:6-8
Learning to be content with nothing more than food and clothing is a desired goal.

11. Luke 12:27-31
Our basic needs are met just as God "clothes" the lilies of the field.

12. 1 John 3:22
Continual obedience to God plays a vital part in answered prayer.

13. Mark 11:24
The power of faith filled prayer is displayed.

15. Exodus 2:16 - 3:1
Moses leaves Egypt and becomes faithful at managing the business of his father-in-law.

16. Luke 21:34
Diligent prayer and guarding against the cares of this life which came ever-so-subtly is exhorted.

17. James 4:3
Prayer may not be answered because of our selfish motives.

18. Proverbs 6:10, 11
Lack of discipline and diligence can bring about "overnight" poverty.

19. Malachi 3:8-11
Failing to acknowledge God's ownership gives the "devourer" grounds to affect our financial well-being.

20. Ephesians 1:17, 18
God's design for us to be increasingly spiritually enlightened

21. II Corinthians 6:4-10
God brings us to deeper commitment and more effective ministry to others through difficulties and even through the absence of material security

22. James 1:4
Patience opens doors for supernatural results (even in finances)

23. Ephesians 2:4-7
God's desire to show us eternally the richness of His grace toward us

24. Proverbs 16:19, 20
A humble dependence upon the Lord is far more to be desired than deceptive riches

25. Luke 14:28
Count the cost before initiating a project

26. I Corinthians 6:12
We are not to be under the dominion of earthly habits.

27. I Peter 4:12, 13
Trials in life are to build our Christian character is an indicator of true spiritual commitment.

29. Ecclesiastes 2:4-11
The frustration of the emptiness of world achievements apart from God.

30. Matthew 13:22
Deceitfulness of riches can choke off application of God's Word.

31. 2 Timothy 3:1-7
Description of corruption of “last days” life on earth.

32. Psalm 32:8
God's promise of careful guidance of our lives.

33. Psalm 119:105
The Light of God's Word our supernatural guide through this earthly life.

34. III John 2
The Apostle's wish that God's children experience health and prosperity.

35. Joshua 1:8, 9
Meditating on and obeying His Word means success and prosperity.

36. Proverbs 10:22

God's blessing can bring joy-filled prosperity.

37. Proverbs 22:29

Diligence in work will mean great personal fulfillment.

38. Psalm 23:1 -

The Lord is my Shepherd, I shall not want.

39. Philippians 4:16-19

God's promise of earthly provision for His children.

Let's Get Personal !

1. Why does God often use money to force us to reevaluate our spiritual status?

2. What are the benefits of the absence of financial security or stability?

3. Give one example in your life of a financial crisis that brought you closer to God.

"HON I WANT YOU TO KNOW THAT NOW I KNOW JUST HOW YOU FEEL."

Chapter Six

Blessed Battle Scars

It was a cold December night. I was on my way to a Christmas party at Bill and Melinda's home. Rachel was home with sick little Ben. I was hardly in the mood for the holiday celebration I was about to attend.

It was during the latter months of my two-year mysterious illness that God led us to start a Bible teaching church in an area of suburban Atlanta which needed such a ministry. He had clearly led us to vary our philosophy of ministry considerably from traditional church programs. For the first two years it appeared that mighty things were destined for that lively body of believers. In the months preceding this Christmas season, however, the church had taken a dramatic nosedive as far as attendance was concerned. Some of the families had left because they felt that I, as the pastor, had not performed as expected. Others claimed we had an inadequate youth program. And, finally, some left because others were leaving and they thought, "surely something must be wrong".

To varying degrees, the criticisms were correct. Some of those who had left - including a few whom we had known for years - were quite verbal in their criticisms. The direct criticism wasn't so bad, but the wounds really got deep when we started hearing it second and third and fourth hand. Naturally, we would have preferred to have heard, "Pastor, I know you are going through a difficult time and I have asked God to use me and my family as a special source of help and encouragement to you during the next few months." Or even, "Pastor, we have prayed much about this, and we are absolutely positive that God is leading us to seek fellowship in another church."

To put it quite mildly, we were heartbroken. Though much of the hurt inflicted was not intended, we had never before experienced this depth of discouragement. In time, though, the worst passed and God began His patient rehabilitation program in our lives. Rachel and I were, with His help, beginning to "forget those things which were behind and to reach forward to what lay ahead". But I did not need reminding that many of those who had left the church would be attending that Christmas get together and, what an utterly helpless feeling came over me. "Lord, please lift me out of this despondency. I desperately need your encouragement!"

ANTICIPATING CONFLICT

As the miles of pavement passed on the way to the party, the faces of those who would be there came to my mind one by one.

Try as I did, nothing could keep me from thinking about those people. Before that memorable evening was to come to an end, God was to show me why each of those individuals was brought before my mind's eyes.

Herb and Doris would be there. Herb had called me long distance five years before and asked my assistance during a difficult time in his ministry. Six months of prayer, hard work and miracles later, the ministry was relocated here in Atlanta and really beginning to flourish. Buz and Kathy would be there. They were working with Herb's ministry, and we had helped them get settled in their very first home. Doc and Mindy would be there, too. They later came to work with Herb and taught a children's class in our church.

Mel and Harriet would be there. Mel and I had started a Christian printing business together. The business eventually came to an end, but we remained friends and still have a good laugh about our old sinking ship. Tim and Nancy would come. I was the one who kept leaving the "we are praying for you" notes on their door while their two baby girls underwent life-or-death surgery. Years later they joined our church.

Ben and Pat were probably invited. Ben was won to Christ through our church ministry after a lifetime of alcoholism. What a miracle! Jim and Nancy might attend. I'll never forget meeting Jim. His Christian partner had just finagled Jim's business right out of his hands. He wanted nothing to do with Christianity! Several games of golf and a genuine friendship later, Jim was a growing Christian.

Rick and Vivian would probably come also. They had just

begun building their very first home in our little Christian community. Carl and June would surely be there. Carl taught a Biblically-rich seminar called *Spiritual Dynamics*. His family of four moved into our home for seven months while the seminar material was being assembled. Our two families lived on $35.00 a week for groceries. What a miraculous experience!

Tom and Bobbi might attend. They had just been born into God's family one year before on Easter Sunday and were our good friends. Ed and Beverly would be invited. Rachel had befriended Beverly during a crisis time in her life and they had grown close. Ben and Cynde were surely invited. Years before they had come to live with us during a trying time in their lives. Will and Carolyn would come. What a joy to be their pastor when their first child arrived.

Though the evening's events went smoothly, that gnawing, empty feeling never left for a moment. Later, as I pulled out of the driveway to return home I again sensed an urgent need for God's comfort and loving kindness! "Lord, I am calling upon You in a time of need. I need your presence!" And He was there when I needed Him. As if He were sitting next to me in the passenger's seat (to this day, I could not be otherwise convinced), this very clear message was divinely transmitted: People - that's what it is all about. You keep reaching out to them and let Me be concerned with the results.

God had graciously used Rachel and me in a small way to touch the lives of every one of those individuals who came to my mind on the way there. Many of them had ministered to us in a special way. Whether they had left the church quietly or critically or never attended at all was not to be our primary concern. We were simply to continue to allow Him to touch through us as many lives as He would. A warm assurance and love literally hugged my soul! "Thank you, Lord. Great is Thy Faithfulness."

Friends,
we're to be responsible
for each other's growth
and improvement.
We have to care.
We have to stick
with each other until it happens.
in a divided world,
believers must demonstrate
how God can put people together.
You can't be right
in your doctrine
and wrong in your living!

Anne Ortlund

PEOPLE PROBLEMS

People. They can love and they can hurt. They can be beautiful and they can be downright ugly. But we must, as His ambassadors, keep on loving them; and we must, we must, we must, become increasingly sensitive to how God would have us grow and profit through life's ever plentiful and often traumatic experiences.

Indeed, people pressures and people-hurts are one of life's genuine hard spots. The mind keeps thinking, "Maybe, tomorrow, the hurt will go away". Tomorrow comes and still the hurt. "Next week? Next month? Next year? Ever?" Yes, though ever so gradually, those seemingly devastating wounds do begin to heal. And, during that healing process, our heavenly Father never fails to provide some unexpected source of comfort for those unfillable empty places in our hearts.

How would the Lord have us respond to these hurts and disappointments? Certainly our human tendencies in the face of people-hurts will likely be attitudes of bitterness and despondency. Undeniably, though, our Lord's desire is that we draw close to Him, experiencing more intimately His matchless friendship. His will is that: "It is better to take refuge in the Lord than to trust in man. It is better to take refuge in the Lord than to trust in princes." (Psalm 118:8,9) "Though a host should encamp against me, my heart will not fear; though war rise against me, in spite of this I shall be confident." (Psalm 27:3) "Humble yourselves, therefore, under the mighty hand of God, that He may exalt you at the proper time, casting all your anxiety upon Him, because He cares for you." (1 Peter 5:6,7)

You might be asking, "Since I ought to be casting my cares (people-hurts included) upon Him, is it a sin that I just seem to keep on hurting?" I think not - for this reason: as one studies the lives of the men and women of faith in the Bible and particularly the experiences of the nation of Israel - it is clear that the pains of defeat and disappointment often did not disappear overnight - perhaps as a continuing reminder that their confidence, their source of strength, their emotional stability, should be forever resting in Him! (Genesis 25:42)

So, too, with us today. How quickly and unknowingly we begin to look to people rather than to the Lord for the external help and the internal uplifting we need day by day. God sometimes allows people to disappoint us in order to bring us back into proper perspective; prompting us to realize once again that life's answers are not in this world, but in Him!

"What if these disappointing people failures are my fault to begin with?" is very often the next question asked. David's openness before the Lord provides the answer. "Search me, 0 God, and know my heart, try me and know my thoughts; and see if there be any hurtful way in me, and lead me in the everlasting way." (Psalm 139:23)

So is that all there is to it? Are we simply to ask God to reveal our wrong attitudes and actions that may have prompted people conflicts, and confess that sin to Him and go about our business? Not always. For the business He wills for us may be the task of reconciliation; the kind of reconciliation we see so vividly illustrated in the life of the patriarch Jacob.

JACOB - FROM CONSCIENCE TO CONVICTION

Jacob had, in quite a masterful plot of deceit, stolen away his brother Esau's elder son privileges. You can imagine how this act of trickery must have plagued Jacob's mind over the ensuing years. A reconciliation must be made! And God resourcefully arranged that opportunity through an amazing series of circumstances.

After twenty years of separation, an emotional reunion between Jacob and the brother he had defrauded occurred. He (Jacob) passed on ahead of them and bowed down to the ground seven times, until he came near to his brother. Then Esau ran to meet him and embraced him, and fell on his neck and kissed him, and they wept. And he said, "What do you mean by this company which I have met? And he said, 'To find favor in the sight of my lord.' But Esau said, 'I have plenty, my brother, let what you have be your own.' And Jacob said, 'No, please, if now I have found favor in your sight, then take my present from my hand, for I see your face as one sees the face of God, and you have received me favorably.' " (Genesis 33:8-10)

That kind of humbling, however, may also be God's design in times when we are not at fault. Our desire to make things right (especially when we may not be at fault) with a friend or loved one is one of life's really difficult tasks: "And the Lord's bond-servant must not be quarrelsome, but be kind to all, able to teach, patient when wronged, with gentleness correcting those who are in opposition, if perhaps God may grant them repentance leading to the knowledge of the truth, and they may come to their senses and escape from the snare of the devil, having been held captive by him to do his will."(Genesis 33) "For this finds favor, if for the sake of conscience toward God a man bears up under sorrows when suffering unjustly. For what credit is there if, when you sin and are harshly treated you endure it with patience? But if when you do what is right and suffer for it you patiently endure it, this finds favor with God." (1 Peter 2:19-20)

So, am I to believe that as long as there are people relationships I can expect anything from beautiful and rewarding to ugly and disappointing? Am I to take the good with the bad? Where possible, I should endeavor to make things right with others, and try not to slip into bitterness but hope for the best.

On the contrary, rather than just hoping for the best, why not allow your heavenly Father the opportunity to use difficult relationships as an integral part of molding you into the radiant, Spirit-controlled, tender-tough child He wants you to become?

"God wants us to have tough skins and tender hearts."

And, certainly, people pressures can make us tough while being increasingly tenderhearted! A balance of the two is vital. Here are some of the ways God might allow people - negative characteristics included - to prompt our lives toward a greater depth of spiritual maturity.

ENCOURAGEMENT BUILDS STRENGTH

The root definition of the very name Barnabas means to attend to and uplift. As far as we know, Barnabas never headed up any international Bible colleges, seminaries or Christian organizations! In fact, he may not have even possessed the charisma one might expect to find in the companion of the fervent apostle Paul. But Barnabas was the steadfast, servant-minded kind of person God chose to use to uplift and comfort the key human figure in the world-wide evangelization of the early church age.

What we must remember about encouragement, though, is that it takes at least two to make it work: someone to encourage and uplift and someone to receive and respond to that exhortation. All through his epistles we find that Paul was especially sensitive to, and infinitely grateful for, the encouragement he had received from fellow believers. Let us be willing to be used as an instrument of the Lord in this area - as a giver and as a receiver of one of life's truly vital qualities - encouragement. "Take care, brethren, lest there should be in any one of you an evil, unbelieving heart, in falling away from the living God. But encourage one another day after day. As long as it is still called today, lest any one of you be hardened by the deceitfulness of sin." (Hebrews 3:12,13)

DISCOURAGEMENT WHICH BUILDS FAITH

Job got plenty of this. A quadruple dose to be exact! His embittered wife started the ball rolling by telling Job to "curse God and die." Next came Job's three acquaintances, Elipaz, Bildad and Zophar, each claiming to be a much needed friend. They had come to "comfort" him in his grave afflictions! Rather than comfort him, they literally bombarded Job with words of condemnation and assumptions that his calamities were a sure sign of grave personal sin. After days of listening to such frail human reasoning, Job, in obvious exasperation, answers their "counsel," "Truly then you are the people, and with you wisdom will die! (I have heard many such things; Sorry comforters are you all. Is there no limit to windy words? Or what plagues you that you answer?" (Job 12:2)

"I too could speak like you, if I were in your place. I could compose words against you, and shake my head at you." (Job 16:2-4) "How long will you torment me, and crush me with words? These ten times you have insulted me, you are not ashamed to wrong me. Even if I have truly erred, my error lodges with me." (Job 19:2,3)

"What a help you are to the weak! How you have saved the arm without strength! What counsel you have given to one without wisdom! What helpful insight you have abundantly provided !" (Job 26:2,3)

Talk about having it rubbed in! Talk about having friends disappoint you! Talk about feeling all alone! Did God allow Job's wife and supposed friends to so gravely disappoint him in meaningless belittlement? Quite the contrary. For you will remember at the end of his phenomenal ordeal, Job was rewarded with double of all that he had lost.

What was the apparent key, though, that allowed God to bring Job out of his infirmity and discouragement and into great victory and blessing? Job would seem to have had every reason to have lapsed into a lifetime of bitterness and resentment. Instead, his far different response is recorded in this remarkable record. The Lord restored the fortunes of Job when he prayed for his friends, and the Lord restored the fortunes of Job twofold.

Look at that again. When Job prayed for his friends even though they weren't true friends and were, instead, a real source of discouragement to him, the Lord restored his fortunes. One of the hardest things you may ever do is pray for those who have hurt and disappointed you, but it may be the key to releasing you from the bondage of bitterness. You cannot depend on your feelings; you must do it as an act of faith and obedience. The results, however, may surprise you!

CONFLICTS WHICH BUILD PATIENCE

What an intriguing difference we find in scripture between Acts 15 and 2 Timothy 4. John Mark had apparently deserted Paul and Barnabas during their first missionary journey. This was no small source of irritation to the apostle Paul, for he emphatically refused in spite of the many pleas of his companion, Barnabas, to allow John Mark to accompany them on a later journey.

Years later, however, a still dynamic but much mellowed Paul makes this request to young Timothy: "Only Luke is with me, pick up Mark and bring him with you, for he is useful to me for service." (2 Timothy 4:11) Though Mark was undoubtedly in error in refusing that journey, it is evident that over the years Paul learned that God can change people. Do you give God that much credit? Or, do you just "write people off" as immature, undependable, inconsistent, etc.? You may be the tool God is using to bring about growth in whomever it is that irritates you, but you hinder God's work by your refusal

> "Will we allow annoyances to be a springboard to spiritual growth?

to be in situations that do not bring you pleasure. In the book *Beyond Ourselves*, Catherine Marshall tells of a woman who had not wronged her, but invariably irritated her. She says that her human inclination was to avoid her, but God wouldn't allow that; He insisted on love. Here's how she tells it:

"Love Ann Sheldon? The idea seemed ludicrous. Nevertheless I knew I had to try. First, I recognized that it would have been most unlike Jesus Christ if by 'love' He had meant billowing waves of gushing sentimentality. By love He meant something more substantial: respect for another human being, caring about him and his problems, being sensitive to his needs and wanting him to prosper and to be happy."

"As soon as I faced up to my defective relationship with Ann, I saw that everything turned on my will. I had to be willing to like this woman. Suppose that by some miracle God could replace my irritation with congeniality, even affection? (That would be a miracle, I thought glumly.) But all that God was asking of me was a shift in consciousness at the center of my will to include this possibility . So, in essence, my prayer was, 'Lord, let me admit that my every clamoring emotion rebels at the thought of liking Ann Sheldon! But I put my will over on the side of what is best. So I ask You to handle my feelings.'"

She goes on to tell that God helps her see why this woman behaves as she does, and eventually, a friendship is formed. But she was obedient, even when her emotions dictated otherwise. The question is, are we going to allow these irritations to drive us into despair? Or will we allow these annoyances to be another springboard to spiritual growth, causing us to "Set your mind on things above, not on the things that are on earth." (Colossians 3:2)

If I say, "Yes, I forgive,
but I cannot forget,"
as though the God,
who twice a day
washes all the sands
on all the shores
of all the world,
could not wash
such memories from my mind,
then I know nothing
of Calvary love.

Amy Carmichael

FRIENDSHIPS WHICH PROMPT STEADFASTNESS

My first real lesson in friendship came as a youngster. Our family lived next door to a wise old Dutchman with a robust personality. Uncle Freddie, as I knew him, had a keen insight when it came to people; and he spent an entire lifetime with other people's interests at heart. I will never forget his simple but profound thoughts on friendship: "A friend is someone who, when your little world is crumbling around you, sticks all the closer as things get worse!"

Where, then, are our "friends" when things go from bad to worse"? Why, today, do we see so much more desertion than we do commitment? Is it possible that people today, Christians unfortunately included, have become a people living almost exclusively for their own "best" interests? Has mankind become so self-centered that there just isn't room left one for another? Let us not forget, though, that even those "desertions" can "work together for good." God desires to take even the most painful of broken friendship experiences and build within us a special strength of character that can only be born in pain.

And the ironic thing about it all is that the Lord's promise is that the only really successful way to gain our lives is not to live in self-consumption, but rather to give unreservedly of our time, our resources and, indeed, our friendships. Again, we are faced with that predicament known by definition as choice. Will we continue to live a life of self-centeredness as so well promoted by today's society? Or, will we ask God for the courage and the strength to make the kind of lifelong, selfless commitment Jonathan made with David? The choice is ours; and how profoundly concise God's inspired secretary worded it when he wrote, “A friend loves at all times”.

THE LOCAL CHURCH WHICH BUILDS CHARACTER

In the days shortly after the ascension of Christ, the local assembly of those who had believed on Him was an astonishing group of people with which to be associated: “And all those who had believed were together, and had all things in common; and they began selling their property and possessions, and were sharing them with all, as anyone might have need. And day by day continuing with one mind in the temple, and breaking bread from house to house, they were taking their meals together with gladness and sincerity of heart, praising God, and having favor with all the people. And the Lord was adding to their number day by day those who were being saved.” (Acts 2:42-47)

Unfortunately, this kind of love, unselfishness and sensitivity to God's Spirit gradually begins to wax cold, and today we find far too little of what was taking place in the early church. We must not, however, allow ourselves to forget the remarkable example of New Testament Christianity God chose to leave for us in His Holy Word.

And what do we find in today's church? We often find good preaching, uplifting music, encouraging relationships and a real sense of belonging. Often, though, we might also find: jealousy, envy, backbiting and strife. Do we, therefore, abandon today's church, and perhaps even the particular local assembly to which we belong, in search of the “utopian Christianity” we see recorded of the early church? I believe not. We need to ask ourselves, “Is it not even a slight possibility that the church where I have been attending - the one with the off balance emphasis, with immature people and a pastor who needs vast improvement is the very place God desires to mature me? Faithful wounds, persistent pains, and endless frustrations developed within me a blessed quality called Christlikeness!"

"Speaking the truth in love, we are to grow up in all aspects into Him, who is the head, even Christ, from whom the whole body, being fitted and held together by that which every joint supplies, according to the proper working of each individual part, causes the growth of the body for the building up of itself." (Eph 4:15-16)

Do we want a robot for a friend? A monastery life for a family? A television church for fellowship? That's not the answer! For the price one may pay in hurt and disappointment is more than worth the blessing and enrichment meaningful relationships with fellow believers are ultimately guaranteed to bring.

ONE SMALL TRUTH

What, then, is the conclusion of this matter of people, and the part they are to play in my spiritual growth? If I have learned one "small" truth from my years of ministering, and being ministered to, as a businessman, associate pastor, pastor and ministry administrator, it is this: People. I must keep trusting them and looking for the best from them. People. I must keep loving and reaching out to them as unto the Lord. And, yes, people. Trust them, love them, help them but don't look to them to meet needs in your life that God alone desires to meet.

For those you think to be your dearest friends may desert you quickest; while those you think don't care, do indeed care. Those you are positive will go on in dynamic service for Christ often fail miserably; while the one you least expect to mature spiritually becomes a tower of strength. When the going gets tough and you are just positive you know the human instrument God will use to minister in your behalf, your sure predictions often fail to come true, while your gracious Heavenly Father surprises you with help and comfort through a source that you never would have imagined.

And, just think. God has a purpose to be fulfilled in our contact with every single person whose life we touch. Our life of faith ought to prompt non-Christians to seek the Savior, spur backslidden Christians to restore fellowship with their Lord and encourage growing Christians to mature even more!

The helps and the hurts, the encouragements and the discouragements, the companionships and the desertions, the unity and the strifes are all there to take us a step further. A step further in the lifelong "conformity to His Son" program in which God has enrolled every one of His children. May we have the wisdom and the grace to learn well.

CHAPTER SIX
Verse Summaries

1 . Psalm 118:8-9
It is better to trust in the Lord than to put confidence in man.

2. Psalm 27:3
Though a multitude turns against me, my heart need not fear.

3. 1 Peter 5:6-7
Because of God's unfathomable love for me, my every care can be entrusted to Him.

4. Genesis 25-42
Jacob's growth toward becoming a man of faith.

5. Psalm 139:23
David asks God to search him and test his inner motives.

6. Acts 2:44-47
The closeness of fellowship of the early church is recounted.

7. Ephesians 4:14-16
The strength of doctrine, love and the marvelous interworking of the body of Christ is taught.

8. John 17:20-23
Christ's prayer to the Father for supernatural unity among believers.

9. 1 Corinthians 12

The gifts to the believer are divinely given that the body of Christ might function in supernatural harmony.

10. Galatians 6:1-10

Every believer is responsible to: a) sow the seeds of ministry in other people's lives; b) admonish a weaker, erring brother; c) uplift others in times of need; d) reach out especially to fellow believers.

11. Genesis 33

Miraculous reunion of Jacob and Esau is told.

12. 2 Timothy 2:24-26

The servant of the Lord is to minister graciously to those caught in Satan's snare.

13. Matthew 18:15-22

In the case of a personal conflict, go directly to your brother. Forgive your brother at least 490 times.

14. Galatians 6:1

The spiritual Christian is commanded to, in meekness, restore to fellowship one who has slipped into sin.

15. Ephesians 4:1-3

We are to get along with each other through Christ's love, always endeavoring to bring about unity.

16. 1 Peter 2:19-25

People pressures and false accusations are to turn us toward Him who suffered so for us.

17. Luke 10:30-34
The remarkable account of The Good Samaritan.

18. 2 Timothy 4
The importance of “battling” as a pilgrim in a strange land.

19. Acts 13-15
History of the missionary journey of Paul and Barnabas.

20. Hebrews 3:12, 13
We believers are commanded to encourage one another daily.

21. James 5:16
The power of prayer in the lives of others is clearly illustrated.

22. Romans 15:1-3
Our goal: to be an encouragement to others.

23. Job 12:2
Job's frustration at the “encouragement” of his friends.

24. Job 16:2-4
Job's frustration continues.

25. Job 19:2, 3
Job is crushed by the supposed “exhortation” of his friends.

26. Job 26:2, 3
In exasperation, Job begins to mock his friends' "wisdom".

27. Job 42: 10
Job is miraculously restored twice what he had.

28. 2 Timothy 4:11
Paul requests that Mark be sent to assist him in his ministry.

29. Colossians 3:1-4
Christ, our indwelling life, is the great motivation for our heavenward attention.

30. Proverbs 18:24
Further insight into the demands of friendship.

31. Proverbs I 7:17a
The vitalness of consistency in friendship.

32. Proverbs 27:9
A look into the blessings friendship can bring.

33. Acts 4:32-34
The remarkable unselfishness of the early church is viewed.

O what peace we often forfeit
O what needless pain we bear
All because we do not carry
Everything to God in prayer.

Can we find a friend so faithful
Who will all our sorrows share?
Jesus knows our every weakness
Take it to the Lord in prayer.

Do thy friends despise,
forsake Thee?
Take it to the Lord in prayer
In His arms
He'll take and shield thee
Thou wilt find a solace there.

Joseph Scriven

Let's Get Personal !

1. List at least one reason that broken relationships don't always heal overnight.

2. List any persons (by code or abbreviation) that you need to restore relationship with.

3. Tell how a conflict in your life was used by the Lord to deepen your faith.

LORD, IT DOESN'T LESSEN THE PAIN A WHOLE LOT, BUT I HAVE TO ADMIT THAT KNOWING WHERE I'M HEADED THROUGH THIS EXPERIENCE IS REALLY ENCOURAGING
THE HIGHWAY
OF LIFE

Chapter Seven

Rock Bottom and Somewhere To Go

Four years can be an awfully long time, especially when you are falling flat on your face when you are attempting to do what you are ideally suited for.

This particular morning seemed to me to be far bleaker inside our little church chapel than outside in the wintry landscape. Just a few short months before, nearly one hundred of God's children had gathered on such a Sunday for a victorious time of worship and praising God for His wonderful blessings for the growing church He had given us.

Today was quite different. Three people sat among the rows of empty chairs - each one feeling more nervous for me than for their own conspicuousness. To help fill up the vacant seats, we brought in the crowd from junior church, my three children and their teacher (and mother)! Bless their hearts. Those kids sang as loudly as they could, looked as adult as they could and did their best to encourage their dad in his suppressed disappointment.

After all, I had been sure this was my life work. I was supposed to be building a future for my family. A lifelong, fulfilling career. A successful ministry. And the worst part of it was that the ingredients appeared to be right. I seemed to be a reasonably good organizer, a man of vision and at least adequate in pastoral skills. Rachel was a gifted musician and teacher with a lifetime of ministry experience as a missionary's daughter.

Something wasn't right, though. And, as the weeks passed, God began to unfold to us what was to be an amazing revelation. While the declining numbers of the church prompted some real soul searching, God was wonderfully, tenderly at work in revealing to us both His ways and our limitations.

As I travel and meet Christians from all walks of life who have experienced varying degrees of career failures, one truth has become undeniably evident: being a Christian is not an automatic assurance that God will make us successful in a field in which we have natural ability.

In a survey I have been conducting among Christians the response to questions concerning attitudes towards career has brought an interesting response. I'm finding that most believers are not really content with their careers. More crucial, however, is that a surprising percentage label themselves as lifelong career failures, often believing that they really are not cut out for any specific life profession.

The devastating part about that kind of thinking is that God becomes handcuffed. For as long as one is consumed with his own limitations and inadequacies, he is blinded to the wonderful character and skills God is desiring to build in him through that failure.

For even as we are finding ourselves inundated in career failures and disappointments God is at work preparing us spiritually and emotionally for the future. And don't limit your future with God! The possibilities are as limitless as the mind of God - regardless of your age, number of children, or quantity of impossibilities.

A man whom I know had planned early in his career to go to South America as a missionary, but through prejudice and an unfair judgment by the board of the mission he was serving, he was not allowed to go. In fact, he was told his services were not needed. (He never did tell me this story, by the way, but a friend of his did.) For he never became bitter but always said that "God had closed the door." Soon after that disappointing rejection he was hired to be the director of a home mission, and served there contentedly for many years. Twenty years later, his mission's governing board voted to rescue and keep afloat a struggling ministry in South America. You guessed it! It was the same mission that had refused him twenty years earlier! God had used his failure to accomplish his career goal - just as He had by promoting Joseph up the ladder of the school of tough breaks, so that his family (the seed of God's chosen people) might be saved when the famine came.

We cannot see down the road. God does not give us a crystal ball. Too many Christians believe that whatever God calls them to do they will do all their lives; but many times God will use circumstances to teach us patience or obedience, and then lead us on. We need to be always open to God's leading, and while our friends may think we have failed, or we may think we have failed, we need to remind ourselves that we are led by One who knows the way ahead and who loves us and wants our best. He never leads any two people exactly the same way. "In his heart a man plans his course, but the Lord determines his steps". (Proverbs 16:9)

Many people tend to give up easily (and that can be a problem) but others of us die hard. Our pride will not allow us to be open to that "still, small voice" because of what people might say. So God must bring into our lives a series of failures. And depending on how hard-headed we are, He will continue to apply pressure until we say uncle.

Or in this case, "Yes, Lord." In my life, God would not allow me to quit (which I certainly wanted to do) after that humiliating Sunday. He did use that circumstance to begin to lead me into another ministry. My years of pastoral experience were not in vain in the Lord. God would use that training those hurts and disappointments included - to bring encouragement into the lives of others including many who read and studied the first printing of this book.

So what do you do when you are experiencing career failures? Fall back on the Lord for wisdom! Ask Him if you are being unwise in any aspect of the business. Listen for instructions and tell the Lord that you will do whatever He tells you to do. Then seek the Lord for the grace and patience to continue to grow spiritually - even though the circumstances may dictate bitter resentment and discouragement.

Remember that God is more patient with you than you likely are with yourself. Commit your abilities as well as your inabilities to the Lord and allow Him, in His flawless timing, to use circumstances, failures, successes and even career frustrations to bring you to vocational maturity. God is interested in your future, and He desires fulfillment in every area of your life.

Remember, too, that God is never in a hurry. " 'For my thoughts are not your thoughts, neither are your ways my ways,' declares the Lord. 'As the heavens are higher than the earth, so are my ways higher than your ways and my thoughts than your thoughts.' " (Isaiah 55:8,9) "Perseverance must finish its work so that you may be mature and complete, not lacking anything." (James 1:4)

May God give us the grace and the strength to give thanks in the face of even the most devastating of our career failures. And, may He grant us the divine eyesight to see His hand of correction, direction and confirmation through those experiences. (Colossians 1:10-12)

There are a myriad of disappointments, however, that may take us further than discouragement. How quickly disappointment can turn to discouragement which, if unchecked, may become depression. "You mean to tell me there is beauty, even in depression?" Let's move on and see!

DEALING WITH THE DOLDRUMS

Depression. There is nothing quite like it. And it is especially devastating to someone who has spent over thirty years of his life with a very positive attitude. I was there! Was I ever! Business, friend, family and ministry failures all seemed to catch up with me in one frightening avalanche of frustration.

Life's heartaches had taken their toll. No one needed to convince me that my spiritually and emotionally low state did not show evidence of depression. I knew in theory that when life's trials were to overtake me, God was more than able to graciously comfort and encourage even me. But theory wasn't working very well! Was I to be the exception to the scriptural rules of victory through faith?

Where did Savonarola
get his eloquence?
In the darkness
and the burning of the furnace
wherein God revealed
deep things to him.
Where did Stradavari
get his violins?
Where did Titian get his color?
Where did Angelo get his marble?
Where did Mozart get his music,
and Chatterton his poetry,
and Jeremiah his sermons?
They got them where the clay
gets its glory and its shimmer —
in the darkness
and the burning of the furnace.

Robert G. Lee

Had I dipped too deep into discouragement for His Spirit to revitalize my despondent spirit? For nothing - that I said or did or thought - seemed even to hint at bringing me out of my depressed state. I had virtually no desire to study the Bible, to be around fellow Christians or to perform in my occupation. More disheartening still, there were even days upon end when I didn't even care that I didn't care! For months it haunted me. Marriage, children, friendships and ministry were all acutely influenced by it.

God did not change my circumstances. Neither did He send a supernatural revelation from heaven. Nor did He instantaneously replace that despondency with an overwhelming joy. Assuredly, He was at work. How many times I remember saying, "God, I don't want to feel like this. I don't want to not care. I desire to have the motivation to study Your Word, to be of encouragement to my family and friends, and to again experience your joy. But, Lord, you are going to have to work miraculously in me to bring back those desires because, of myself. I simply cannot."

I'm convinced that those "I cannot, please help me" kind of conversations with the Lord are exactly what He was awaiting. For it was when I became consumed with my own problems and disappointments - consistently looking inward at my own unfortunate predicaments rather than upward toward my victorious Lord - that the wiles of depression had overpowering access into my life. My cry of helplessness was the first step to climbing out of that depressed state.

"My cry of helplessness was the first step to climbing out of that depressed state."

"I cannot, you can, please do!" It was this kind of broken-ness that God used in David's life when he said, "The sacrifices of God are a broken spirit; A broken and a contrite heart, O God, Thou wilt not despise." (Psalm 51:17)

OUT OF THE DOLDRUMS

For ever so patiently, in divine tenderness, my heavenly Father began to minister to me - faithfully instilling again that hunger for His truths. Love for family and friends inched its way back into my emotional being. Joy, so unlike anything this world can offer, gradually reappeared.

Looking back on those very dark months I see one of the really frightening aspects of being depressed is that a person experiencing it is certain it will never leave! I surely felt that way. Since then I always make it a point to really encourage people not to give up on themselves or their future - no matter how hopeless it may appear.

Think of it. We have a God who is personally interested in ministering to our innermost needs. One who is absolutely able to meet the profoundest of those longings! "0h Lord, you have searched me and you know me. You know when I sit and when I rise; you perceive my thoughts from afar. You discern my going out and my lying down; you are familiar with all my ways. Before a word is on my tongue you know it completely, O Lord." (Psalm 139:1-4) "For we do not have a high priest who is unable to sympathize with our weaknesses, but we have one who has been tempted in every way, just as we are - yet was without sin." (Hebrews 4:15)

This is not to say that dealing with depression is a simple matter. Its causes are numerous. Its grip is tenacious. Its long-range consequences can be devastating. One's conceding to a lifetime of despairing defeatism is denying the limitless healing resources of an ever-loving God.

"I sought the Lord, and He answered me; he delivered me from all my fears. Those who look to him are radiant; their faces are never covered with shame. This poor man called, and the Lord heard him; he saved him out of all his troubles. The angel of the Lord encamps around those who fear him, and he delivers them. Taste and see that the Lord is good; blessed is the man who takes refuge in him." (Psalm 34:1-8)

MISSING THE MARK

Most importantly, we need to address the matter of sin. If we were to take a survey of the number one problem in the world today - the problem that wrecks marriages and families, careers and ambitions, causes misunderstandings and wars, and keeps Christians from real joy and prosperity - the answer would be sin. And one way or the other, we are all plagued with sin's ugliness.

Will we allow these defeats to cause us to lapse into a hopeless state of self-pity - convinced that Solomon's dismal conclusions were penned specifically to describe our powerless lives? Or, will we thank God for His forgiveness and cleansing of the sin in our lives and move on (even if it be but "an inch at a time" toward greater levels of spiritual maturity?

It is important to remember, that while we need to acknowledge our sinful actions each day, there is in most of us at least one stronghold of sin. This is what we often call our biggest weakness or our life hang-up. It is a particular area of our thought life, our family life or our daily life that is clearly not under the Spirit's control. In many Christians this sin-stronghold has deep roots. “For sin, seizing the opportunity afforded by the commandment, deceived me, and through the commandment put me to death.” (Romans 7:11) “As it is, it is no longer I myself who do it, but it is sin living in me. I know that nothing good dwells in me, but I cannot carry it out. God lives in me, that is, in my sinful nature. For I have the desire to do what is good, but I cannot carry it out”. (Romans 7:17-18)

Might it be that the apostle Paul's many years of Christian experience are God's way of illustrating to us the absolute tenaciousness of sin? He experienced deep-rooted and difficult to overcome sin problems in his own life, and we certainly do ourselves nothing but harm in failing to face up to our struggles.

"God deals with our ugliness in a wonderful patient manner."

The beautiful side of the picture, though, is that God deals with our inner ugliness in a wonderfully patient manner. As the Great Physician, He exposes our sins to us, encourages us to ask Him to deal with that sin-problem and then initiates divine surgery to begin removal of that troubled area. The surgery may hurt! We may allow the sin to grow back and force our Physician to operate again. But praise His name that He is always far more patient with us than we are with ourselves. And thank Him that He gives us times of recuperation between operations! I'm sure that if all of the wrong attitudes needing removal were revealed to us in one sitting that our minds, emotions and bodies would absolutely come unglued! All that would be left of us would be a pool of jelly on the floor.

God is loving, gracious, longsuffering and simply abounding in tender mercies. He longs for holiness in our lives and His Holy Spirit exercises a firm, but gentle persistence in working in cooperation with us to instill within us these Christ-like qualities. "Therefore, prepare your minds for action; be self-controlled; set your hope fully on the grace to be given you when Jesus Christ is revealed. As obedient children, do not conform to the evil desires you had when you lived in ignorance. But just as he who called you is holy, so be holy in all you do; for it is written: 'Be holy, because I am holy' ". (1 Peter 1:13-16)

CONQUERING THE STRONGHOLDS

A common roadblock in the battle with sin is our tendency to wage the war erratically, one day really depending upon the Spirit's strength for victory while the next day operating in the flesh. But the warfare we are in is with awesome, ruthless, evil influences. As a child of the King we dare not let our guard down. We must continue to be ". . strengthened with might by His Spirit in the inner man." (Ephesians 3:16) keeping sinful thoughts, attitudes and evil habits from dominating our lifestyles. "But flee from these things, you man of God; and pursue righteousness, godliness, faith, love, perseverance and gentleness. Fight the good fight of faith; take hold of the eternal life to which you were called, when you made the good confession in the presence of many witnesses." (1 Timothy 6:11,12)

"Therefore, since we have so great a cloud of witnesses surrounding us, let us also lay aside every encumbrance, and the sin which so easily entangles us, and let us run with endurance the race that is set before us, fixing our eyes on Jesus, the author and perfecter of our faith, who for the joy set before Him endured the cross, despising the shame, and has sat down at the right hand of the throne of God." (Heb 12:1,2)

In summary, we need to be open and honest before the Lord about both our day-by-day sinful actions and the possible strongholds of sin that cause so many spiritual defeats. We then need to acknowledge these sins to Him daily (moment by moment), thanking Him for the cleansing and restoring of fellowship with Him that He brings into our lives through our honest, repentant admittance of sin.

We then begin to "walk in the light as He is in the light", endeavoring by His grace to obey the promptings of His Word and His Spirit rather than the urgings of the fleshly, worldly impulses which still influence our decision-making. If there is within us a stronghold of sin, we need to be daily combating it with the marvelous spiritual weapons God has made available to us. (Ephesians 6:10-20)

Career failures, depression and sin can all be overwhelming, throwing our lives into seeming hopeless ruin. But hopeless they are not! For the God who created the universe is quite able to recreate us, turning even the darkest of those failures into living proof that He is still very much a God of miracles - of making possible the impossible - of doing in our lives "more than we could have ever asked for or even imagined." Praise His Name!

The breaking of our hearts is much like the breaking up of storm clouds in the sky. Only then can God allow the sun to shine through and give evidence of His love through the sign of His covenant - the rainbow.

CHAPTER SEVEN
Verse Summaries

I . Proverbs 16:9

Our steps are ultimately directed by the Lord.

2. Psalm 37: 23, 34

One seeking to please the Lord may fall, but God is soon to lift him back to level ground.

3. Isaiah 6:8

Isaiah's willingness to go whenever and wherever God would send him.

4. 2 Timothy 2:3-7

Much discipline required in career achievement.

5. 1 Corinthians 9:24-27

Every man striving for excellence is self-controlled in every phase of life.

6. 1 Corinthians 4:2

The requirement of the Lord's servant: day by day faithfulness.

7. Galatians 6:7-9

In due time our daily faithfulness will bring blessing and reward.

8. Hebrews 2:17, 18
Christ's understanding of even our deepest frustrations.

9. Genesis 12-22
The building of Abraham's life career.

10. Proverbs 22:29
Disciplined living brings career success.

11. Proverbs 31
The blessing bestowed upon the diligent woman.

12. Psalm 112
Characteristics of a spiritually prosperous man.

13. Jeremiah 1:1-9
God's interest in Jeremiah's life career

14. Philippians 1:6-10
The Lord's promise to continually work in our lives in bringing us to maturity.

15. Isaiah 55:8, 9
The depth of God's doings in our lives is beyond our comprehension.

16. James 1:4
Patience at work brings maturity.

17. Genesis 29-30
Jacob's twenty years of career training.

18. Exodus 2-4
Moses' forty years of career training.

19. 2 Peter 1: 1 -14
Building blocks toward Christian maturity.

20. Colossians 1: 10-12
God desires spiritual maturity in every area of our lives.

21. Psalm 23
The ministry of the Loving Shepherd in the believer's life.

22. Psalm 27:1-7
God's marvelous strength in times of trouble.

23. Psalm 46:1 -11
God is our very present source of refuge and strength.

24. Psalm 119:165
The miraculous serenity that comes from loving His truths.

25. Isaiah 26:3
The peace God gives to those who trust in Him.

26. Isaiah 41:10
Reasons God's children need not fear.

27. Matthew 28:19, 20
Christ's command that we go minister, knowing that He is always with us.

28. Romans 8:28, 29

By understanding God's plan to conform us to Christ's image, we can know He causes things to happen toward our ultimate spiritual and physical good.

29 1 Corinthians 10:11-14

God's commitment never to burden us with more than we can bear.

30. James 1: 1 -12

The blessings of gracefully enduring temptations.

31. Psalm 139:1-4

God's understanding of even our innermost shortcomings.

32. Hebrews 4:15

Christ, our High Priest, understands our hurts and temptations.

33. Book of Psalms

Much of the comfort in Psalms given from the perspective of one enduring much failure, sin and the frustration of personal disappointments.

34. Psalm 34:1-8

God promises deliverance to one who continually seeks after Him.

35. 1 John 1:4-9

The step-by-step progress of walking in the light.

36. Psalm 51:1-12
David's plea for forgiveness, cleansing and restored fellowship with the Lord.

37. John 15:1 -10
The Lord's ministry in our lives purges sin and brings a deeper relationship with Himself.

38. 1 Corinthians 3:1-15
The believer's impending judgment prompts us to spend a life seeking to please Him.

39. Romans 7:11, 17, 18
The example of Paul's lifelong struggle with the awesome power of sin.

40. Romans 7:17-18
In spite of our desire not to succumb to it, sin is a powerful force.

41. 1 Peter 1: 13-16
The Lord's command that we pursue a holy lifestyle

42. Romans 12:1, 2
We are to present our lives as instruments for His service.

43. Ephesians 1:2-21
The power that is in a consecrated life.

44. 2 Timothy 2:19-26
The vitalness of being a vessel fit for the Master's use.

45. Ephesians 3:16
We may be strengthened by the power of the indwelling spirit.

46. 1 Timothy 6:11-12
Paul's exhortation that we "fight the good fight of faith".

47. Hebrews 12:1, 2
Christ is our motivation and strength to put aside the sin and hindrances which so consistently overtake us.

48. 1 John 1:7
Fellowship that comes from walking in the light.

49. Ephesians 6:10-20
List of the believer's spiritual defenses and weapons.

Let's Get Personal !

1. List three human elements that most frequently trigger depression.

2. In the event you experience depression, what scripture would you use for spiritual comfort?

3. List two biblical characters who, despite their seemingly unforgivable sins, overcame those failures to be mightily used by God.

BOY DAD, HAVE I LEARNED SOME LESSONS THAT I WILL NEVER FORGET.

Chapter Eight

Today Is The Only Day

Rachel and I had been preparing ourselves for the moment of truth, expressing our sad good-byes to the people of our church. God had been working marvelously in many lives, some of whom had been with us, through thick and thin, from the founding of the fellowship. We were in the midst of the remodeling of the new sanctuary and were much encouraged by God's faithfulness to keep His " . . in due season you will reap if you do not faint . ." promise that was now being evidenced in so many lives! But it was clear that we were to move on. God had miraculously provided Christian Financial Concepts with the funds to purchase the Hidden Lake Training Center in the North Georgia mountains, and His clearly revealed leading was for me to remain in my administrative position with that ministry.

But another altogether different emotion was mixed in with the sadness of leaving. It was the sheer joy of looking back on God's never-ending faithfulness. On several occasions onlookers had given that little church up for dead. By God's grace, though, it had weathered the storms of pastoral inadequacies, of criticism from without and from within and, more than a few times, the onslaught of my unsuccessful decisions and actions. Yet, there it stood. Nothing flashy. No state attendance records being broken. But people were being reached with the good news of redemption's plan. Believers were maturing. Young people were being trained up in the nurture and admonition of the Lord. God's wonderful truths were being faithfully taught.

I could not help but dwell momentarily on the nearly six years of adventure we had been through with that little body of believers. Thoughts came rapid-fire to mind : of marriages saved by God's supernatural working; of unreachables won to Christ; of the tear-filled burying of a loved one; of watching and helping teenagers grow through those difficult years; of great fellowship at our summer picnic/softball outings; of men's retreats with all night discussions on theology and personal improvement; of watching a handful of families sacrifice to build a church building; of dealing with a demonically-controlled young lady who was prayed for and marvelously delivered; of family retreats in the mountains; of an encouraging word when all seemed to be going wrong; of faithfully attended workday events . . . even in sleet storms and in 110° heat; of personality conflicts dissolved in the love of Christ; of listening to the children learn to sing the great old hymns of the faith; of seeing God use His people resources to feed our families during times of unemployment; of watching God tenderly bring families out of bitterness and into restored fellowship with Him.

How amazing is hindsight! As I look back now on the victories God wrought over those years, I cannot help but praise him for many invaluable learning experiences. One of which is simply, yet profoundly, passed on to us through the inspired writings of that battle-wise but victory-laden old apostle himself. "Therefore, my beloved brethren, be steadfast, immovable, always abounding in the work of the Lord, knowing that your toil is not in vain in the Lord." (1 Cor. 15:58)

There were, as you know, plenty of valleys - the empty church Sundays, the "why don't you quit suggestions", the "we want to quit" days and the struggle filled times of God's "don't you dare quit unless I tell you to do so" admonitions.

Yet, in God's dealings with us through that church those impassable storms were indeed the Heavenly Father's creative working laboratories. We saw how He majestically, omnipotently, seeks to instill a rainbow-like Christ-likeness into the lives of those once proud, who are now broken - once success-filled, now humbled - once self-willed, now submissive. Is not the King of Kings ready to respond to the kind of children who, though they may fall into the mire of failure, get back up . . again . . and again . . and again. "For a righteous man falls seven times, and rises again, But the wicked stumble in time of calamity." (Luke 7:1-10)

These experiences of failure have taught me more than just persistence. Looking back it is quite evident that the circumstances, the pressures, the people and my limitations never changed significantly. I changed! And I continue to do so. God used my failures to instill more of His character in me!

Life is a great mixture of
happiness and tragic storm.
He who comes out of it
rich in living,
is he who dares to accept it all,
face it all,
and let it blow its power,
mystery and tragedy into the
inmost recesses of the soul.
A victory won in this life
will then be an
eternal possession.

Charles Lewis Slattery

God worked a miracle in teaching me to grow through those difficult experiences - even including those I brought on through my own impulsive disobedience. What could have become a decade of bitter memories has actually become a sweetness to my spiritual taste. The potential bitterness which could have easily become the daily fuel for my emotional energy has been transformed, (by Him and Him alone!) into grace - a divine enablement, to press on in life, truly believing that my wonderful, matchless and masterfully skillful Heavenly Father is "working together for good" every detail of my life.

Looking back, each of us should be able to say, "I'm changing. I'm learning to look not so much at the terribleness of my problem but at the greatness of my problem-solver." I'm learning to stop fighting the circumstances and start trusting the omnipotent character builder. I am, by His grace, learning not to react humanly but rather to respond in a godly manner to life's heartaches. These are the attitudes and actions He desires to develop in each of our lives, through the success or failure of whatever circumstance life may bring. "For whom He foreknew, He also predestined to become conformed to the image of His Son, that he might be the first-born among many brethren." (Rom 8:29)

The beauty of God working in our lives, particularly as He works through failure, is threefold. **First,** we can always be assured that God's workings are prompted by His unfathomable love for us - regardless of our weaknesses. (Ephesians 2:1-10) **Second,** there is great comfort in realizing that the same miracle-working God who has in the past so marvelously blessed our obedience to Him, is ready and able to do so again and again and again. **Third,** the character qualities that God is building in our lives will bring us supernatural strength and immeasurable joy. (Philippians 2:16)

Indeed, failure ought to be but a threshold to true spiritual success - success that needs to begin today. For today is the best opportunity we will ever have to begin responding in faith to the assorted circumstances, sufferings, monetary crises, people-pressures, inability-disabilities and sin-failures that are endlessly being hurled our way.

Responding - as did **Enoch,** seeking the minute by minute companionship with His God over the busyness and successes of this world.

As did the **Centurion** who realized that not his earthly power, but Christ's divine power, would bring about supernatural results. (Luke 7:1-10)

As did **Gideon** and his band of three hundred, laying aside impossible circumstances in simple, childlike obedience to God's instructions. (Judges 7,8) As did the **Apostles** as God's instruments in turning the world upside down for the cause of Christ in the face of terrifying dangers. (1 Cor 4:9-13)

As did **Epaphroditus** being mightily used of God in and through the grave infirmity that was upon him. (Phil. 2:21-30) As did **Noah,** looking to God for patience and strength during the one hundred and twenty years of persecution in the building of the Ark. (Genesis 6,7). As did **Hannah**, asking the Lord for courage and a glorious miracle in her prayerful anguish for a son who would bring glory to God. (1 Samuel 1:8-28) As those **martyrs** who were scourged, imprisoned, stoned, destitute, afflicted and tormented for refusing to bow down to temptations and demands of this world. (Hebrews 11:32-40)

As did the **widow** who by giving all that she had, acknowledged to her Lord His complete ownership of not only her possessions but of her rights and expectations as well. (Mark 12:41-44)

As did a lowly herdsman named **Amos,** turning from the enormous people pressures of his day to become the man and the leader God desired of him.

As did **Jonathan,** making sacrificial commitments of loyalty and friendship to his family and to his distressed brother, David. (1 Samuel 18-20).

As did the prophetess **Deborah**, the woman God used to inspire men to fight; and **Barak**, the nobody who was willing (though humanly fearful) to lead - allowing God to divinely overcome in him human inadequacies and uncertainties - that a great victory might be won for their people. (Judges 4). As did **Onesimus,** refusing to allow the guilt and travail of life failures to cause him to lapse into prolonged depression, rather than going forward in positive, profitable service for the Lord. (Philemon). As did the despised little chief of tax collectors, **Zacchaeus**, in acknowledging his sin in the face of ridicule and in committing himself to an entirely transformed lifestyle. (Luke 19:1-10)

FROM THE DUNGEON TO THE PALACE

And, oh, what thrilling evidence we see of God's power over the mighty grasp of defeat and failure in a seldom mentioned Old Testament event: For thirty-seven long years Jehoiachin had existed in a dreary dungeon. Jehoiachin, once a king - a man seemingly in control of his destiny - someone who could say, "I did it my way," (as king he had lived after his own selfish desires) . . and who could buy his way out of most any imaginable problem. During those thirty-seven years he must have experienced countless hours of frustration, defeat and despair.

But then this remarkable series of events occurred: "Now it came about in the thirty-seventh year of the exile of Jehoiachin king of Judah, in the twelfth month, on the twenty-fifth of the month, Meradach, that evil king of Babylon, in the first year of his reign, showed favor to Jehoiachin king of Judah and brought him out of prison. Then he spoke kindly to him and set his throne above the thrones of the kings who were with him in Babylon. So Jehoiachin changed his prison clothes, and had his meals in the king's presence regularly all the days of his life. And for financial support a regular allowance was given him by the king of Babylon, a daily portion all the days of his life until the day of his death." (Jeremiah 52:31-34)

From a dungeon to the king's palace! From despair to unexplainable encouragement! From defeat to glorious deliverance! From ego fulfillment in his own palace to a humble and yet miraculous existence in the royal courtyard of a greater king!

Now Jehoiachin might have insisted on wearing ragged prison garments instead of putting on the clothes the king provided. He might have insisted on a beggar's portion of food, refused to crack a smile in remembrance of life's grave injustices and turned away the king's blessing, insisting he did not deserve such goodness.

I don't believe for a moment that Jehoiachin did that, do you? He experienced a renewed lifestyle! He basked in the king's supernatural provisions, knowing full well that in his own powers he would fail. He took that mighty king at his word and enjoyed his new lease on life! Prison's horrors began to fade as he looked forward to the life that lay ahead.

> **Are you needlessly clinging to the garments of past failures?**

And what about you today? Are you needlessly clinging to the garments of past failures? Are you wallowing in self-pity while the King of Kings invites you to bathe in His tender love? Have you reckoned your life as one of perpetual defeat while your all-powerful heavenly Father asks you to be seated with Him in the heavenlies, (Romans 8:17) high above life's circumstances of despair?

Perhaps there is a desperately needed prison release in your life today! A release from the disappointments, heartaches and defeats of life's often gloomy past. The invitation is extended. The prison doors are unlocked. Life's new garments await you. For yesterday, with either its glorious victories or its miserable defeats, cannot for one instant be relived, revised, or reversed. To worry about it, fret over it or, especially, to let its memories lessen your spiritual stamina, is a disastrous mistake.

Tomorrow? Tomorrow, you say, I will begin to really apply myself spiritually. Tomorrow I'll begin to respond to, rather than stubbornly react to, life's hard spots. Tomorrow, friend, is non-existent. Though it may come today, this very moment is the only time we really have to "number our days", (Psalm 90:12) to “redeem the time”, [Ephesians 5:16] to “walk by faith”, [2 Cor. 5:7] to “grow in grace”, [2 Peter 3:18] to “walk in the light”. [1 John 1:7] “Come now, you who say, ‘Today or tomorrow, we shall go to such and such a city, and spend a year there and engage in business and make a profit.’ Yet you do not know what your life will be like tomorrow. You are just a vapor that appears for a little while and then vanishes away.” [James 4:13,14]

Is failure beautiful? That's really up to you, isn't it? God's end of the “blessed bargain” will be upheld - always! That’s His promise! Do you love Him and desire to live past the failures and present inadequacies that He included for the furtherance of His purposes? If you do, then begin today by allowing Him to again minister to the depths of your soul with these following matchless, mind-boggling truths . . . Think about it. Meditate on it. Believe it. Savor it. Experience it.

“And He who searches the heart knows what the mind of the Spirit is, because He intercedes for the saints according to the will of God. And we know that God causes all things to work together for good to those who love God, to those who are called according to His purpose.” [Romans 8:28]

“Whoever believes that Jesus is the Christ is born of God; and whoever loves the Father loves the child born of Him. By this we know that we love the children of God, when we love God and observe His commandments. For this is the love of God, that we keep His commandments; and His commandments are not burdensome. For whatever is born of God overcomes the world; and this is the victory that has overcome the world, our faith.” [1 John 5:1-4]

Jesus, keep me near the cross

There a precious fountain

Free to all, a healing stream

flows from Calvary's mountain

Near the cross, O lamb of God

Bring its scenes before me

Help me walk from day to day

With its shadow o"er me . .

Till my raptured soul shall find

Rest beyond the river.

Yes, we are in this world, but we need not remain captive to the bondage of this world. As heirs and joint heirs with Christ, we, like King Jehoichin, are living in a foreign land.

Our "natural" home is yet to be experienced. However, we can begin here and now to experience the supernatural reality of His Kingdom.

For as failure in some form or fashion comes strutting our way we may refuse to simply react in human despair as any human would react. We may choose to respond by trusting our King to use this defeat to mold us and bring us a tiny step closer to having the strength of character that a child of the King of Kings ought to have. Indeed, just as King Jehoiachin was miraculously released from physical imprisonment, we may experience deliverance from the enslaving defeat inflicted by life's failures. "But thanks be to God who giveth us the victory through our Lord Jesus Christ." (1 Corinthians 15:58)

Today is the day for you to begin responding Godward, in the splendor of heaven-wrought victory, to the testings of this life ". . . forgetting what lies behind and reaching forward to what lies ahead, I press on toward the goal for the prize of the upward call of God in Christ Jesus." (Phil. 3:14) Amen.

"Today is the day for you to respond to the testings of this life."

THE BEAT GOES ON

It was over a year ago that the last "t" was crossed and the last "i" dotted on the rough draft of "*Reluctant Rainbows*". How it amazes me now as I realize that in my subconscious mind I somehow imagined that with those eight chapters of my life past and written on the pages of a book, I had learned my lessons and might become immune to further feelings of defeat and failure. Nine months after I finished that last chapter, our church, with a new pastor and a building program in progress, was suddenly brought to its knees. Through totally unforeseen and unpredictable events, it shattered in a million pieces. And God made it very clear to Rachel and me that we should not step back in and try again.

After all we had been through in that church, this was the last thing we expected, and it shook us to the very core of our being. On Good Friday I remember thinking that two thousand years before this is how the disciples must have felt. They had invested two to three years of their lives in a cause that fell shattering to their feet as they gazed at the dying Jesus upon the cross. They had hoped He would establish a kingdom, and now He was gone. The grief, the emptiness, the loss of hope must have been excruciating. Then I remembered the words of the song *"Something Beautiful":*

If there ever were dreams that were lofty and noble,
They were my dreams at the start.
And the hopes for lives best were the hopes
that I harbored down deep in my heart.
But my dreams turned to ashes,
my castles all crumbled, my fortunes turned to loss
So I wrapped them all in the rags of my life
And laid them at the cross.

There are no guarantees in this life, there are no hopes realized in this life, there are no dreams fulfilled in this life, except in Christ Jesus.

I realize now that I had become humble in my failure, but I was still proud of the finished product. "It was a struggle, Lord, but we made it didn't we? We finally showed the world how faithfulness pays off." I realize that I could accept my failures as long as I had something to show for it - success at last. I have often thought, "I only have one life, and I want to make it count for Jesus Christ." I wanted something to show for my years of struggle. You know what scripture the Lord showed me?

"But none of these things move me, neither count I my life dear unto myself, so that I might finish my course with joy, and the ministry, which I have received of the Lord Jesus, to testify the gospel of the grace of God." (Acts 24:20)

And I came to experience the meaning of something I had only known before as head knowledge: "To whom God wills to make known what is the riches of the glory of this mystery among the Gentiles, which is: Christ in you, the hope of glory." (Col. 1:27) There is no hope outside of Christ. Christ is in us, that is our only hope of glory -- His life manifested through us. Nothing else matters, everything else falls by the wayside. What a glorious hope we have!

What a glorious future! What a great God!

CHAPTER EIGHT
Verse Summaries

1 . I Corinthians 15:58
We can be steadfast in our labor for Him knowing that it is never in vain.

2. Proverbs 24:16
The God fearing man continues to get back to his feet in spite of great difficulties.

3. Micah 7:7, 8
The prophet's assurance that God will sustain him.

4. Job 1:22 & 13:15
Job's unwavering commitment despite the world caving in around him.

5. Acts 5:27-42
Peter and the other apostles unwavering commitment despite an earlier desertion of their Lord.

6. James 5:7-11
Knowing that our Lord will return we are to have the patience of Job, looking forward to our eternal fellowship with Christ.

7. Romans 8:29
Every child of God is certain to be directed toward Christ-like living.

8. Ephesians 2:1 -10
Splendid summation of the Lords commitment to eternally minister to us.

9. Romans 8: 28, 29
God's supernatural working in using all things to conform us to His Son's likeness.

10. Philippians 2:1-8, 16
Having the mind of a servant as Christ had gives us a wonderful witness to this depraved world.

25. Jeremiah 52:31-34
Summary of Jehoiachin's miraculous release from prison.

26. Romans 8:17
We are joint owners with Christ of all things.

27. Galatians 4:1-7
Our relationship with Christ should revolutionize our lifestyle.

28. 1 John 4:4
Greater is the Christ in us than any force in this world.

29. Matthew 11:28-30
Our Lord's promise for supernatural burden-bearing.

30. Philippians 4:12, 13
His strength enabling us to do the impossible.

31. 1 Corinthians 15:51-58
The resurrected Christ - our guarantee of supernatural enablement.

32. Psalm 90:12
Our days, being limited in number, must be wisely spent.

33. Ephesians 5:16
With much evil influence in this world, we are to use our time for building up of His Kingdom.

34. 11 Corinthians 5:7
We are to walk not by human reasoning but by faith.

35. 11 Peter 3:18
We are to grow in grace and in intimate knowledge of our Lord and Saviour.

36. 1 John 1:7
We are to walk in the light of an ever-strengthening relationship with Christ.

37. James 4:13, 14
God's assurance to us that appears and then vanishes ever so quickly.

38. Romans 8:28
God's promise of trials - turned to blessing even in life's extreme predicaments.

39. I John 5:1-4

The victory which overcomes the onslaught of this world, our faith.

40. 1 Corinthians 15:57

Praise God as He provides us with victory in the person of His Son.

Let's Get Personal !

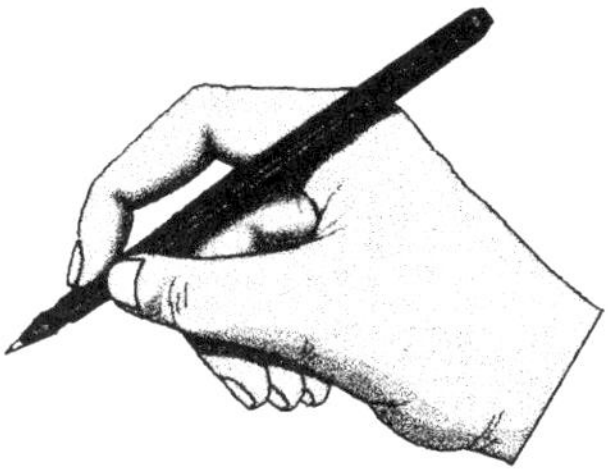

1. Write out your favorite verse of scripture dealing with God's victory over failure in your personal life.

2. Why is it necessary that we learn from and respond to the failures areound us?

3. What methods would you use to minimize past failures and learn to live victoriously?

Lord,
you test me everyday
with all life's
many trials.
I cry to you
to ease the pain
from walking weary miles.

But then I see
your love for me
when every
trial is through;
You care enough
to discipline me
So I will walk closer to you.

Beth Wilson